Things Can Only Get Better

Charles O'Keefe

Things Can Only Get Better Copyright 2022 Charles O'Keefe

Cover art by Kevin Kendall

All rights reserved. The book's authors retain sole copyright to all intellectual contributions to this book, including but not limited to text and images.

Licensed and Produced through
Four Phoenixes Publishing at Createspace
United States Canada United Kingdom

ISBN: 978-1-7750465-5-4

This is a work of non-fiction. All ideas are the author's own.

Table of Contents

Foreword

Chapter 1: My Thoughts on Writing 1
Chapter 2: The Environment 8
Chapter 3: Conventions 16
Chapter 4: Children 24
Chapter 5: COVID and the Pandemic 31
Chapter 6: Travel 39
Chapter 7: University 48
Chapter 8: The Internet 57
Chapter 9: Role-Playing Games 64
Chapter 10: Cycling 73
Chapter 11: Musical Medicine 79
Chapter 12: Relationships 87
Chapter 13: I'm Proud to be a Newfoundlander 93
Chapter 14: The importance of Being Vegetarian. 102
Chapter 15: Losing a Parent 107
Chapter 16: The Geeks Will Inherit the Earth 116
Epilogue: I've Learned a Few Things About Life 123
Appendix A 127
References 131
Acknowledgements 145

About the Author: Charles O'Keefe

Foreword

If you have read my books—and I am flattered if this is the case—then you know I haven't written non-fiction before. I thought my first non-fiction book would be about my dad, but I am had a hard time getting any interviews done, and I've got the writing itch. With time to myself during the pandemic I wanted to write about topics that matter to me and how I think the world severely needs our attention.

I have been told I'm very opinionated and I wouldn't disagree, so it goes without saying that there will be lots of ideas in this book you don't like, agree with, or can't even remotely understand why a sane person would think that way. You may get offended by something I said, and if you want to contact me (and be civil about it) I welcome a discussion on any topic herein. The important point of this whole book is that life is short, don't focus so much on the negative, move on. I'm not saying there aren't ways to make our lives and the world better, in fact, a lot of this book contains my views on how to do precisely that (in theory at least). My point is that while hundreds of things during any given day could bother you, about ninety percent (or more) of them do not matter.

In case you wonder if I have any authority on any of these topics, I did study English, Philosophy, Religion, Folklore, Political Science, (even Business) in university. I have a Masters (and Diploma) in Education along with a few years of teaching experience. I know that sounds like bragging but the only point I am making is I have spent a lot of time thinking and know a bit about some academic subjects. I also have been a vegetarian for fifteen years and have cared deeply about animals for much longer. I'm married and have been for over sixteen years and I have a deep, lifelong love of music, comics, books and other geeky things. I have been fortunate enough to travel to many places and I've certainly had discussions with all kinds of people, many of whom had completely different views than my own. I love to talk, and I have done my best to stay in touch with the world and people in my life.

The thing I think of as most important of all is that while this book is full of the problems I see in the world, I think it's also just as full of the things that bring me joy and what I think we can do to help this wounded, suffering planet. Every day I try to be the best version of myself (and yes, I know that sounds corny as hell). On a lot of days people do not measure up to their own expectations, but I find that if even if I come close just a couple of days a week, it makes it all worthwhile.

On a technical side, it is worth nothing that these chapters are not written in chronological order. Some will refer to events in 2020, other in 2021, as such the chapter on COVID has information that is by no means current. I wanted to keep the feeling I had when the chapter was written (in many cases) and therefore pass along that experience to the reader. As such I am leaving the chapters as is, as George from Seinfeld would say do otherwise would compromise my "artistic integrity!"

So, if you love, hate, or feel somewhere in-between about this book then it was successful. I wanted this book to provoke a reaction in you, to make you give a second thought as to why you have always done something. If I'm being fully honest, even if this book gives a few chuckles or makes you say, "hmm.", "huh?", or even "No way!", then that's all I could hope for. Live life a day at a time and try to make the world a little better around you. That is all most of us can do. Or just read this book to see some ideas this eccentric guy wrote down. It took over eight months to write this and brought me a lot of joy and introspection. I hope it gives a little of both to you.

Chapter 1: My Thoughts on Writing

I know. How cliché can you get; another author talking about writing. In my defense it's only one chapter and something I love, so it's just natural to talk about it. A writer is someone who has written a book, short-story, poem, blog post or even a journal entry. The distinction (which matters for some people) is whether you have something you have written published (either by yourself or someone else), then you are an author. When I think back, I first started to enjoy writing somewhere around the time I was ten years old, when I wrote some story about the Transformers as a school project. After that, I remember at age twelve or thirteen I wrote stories about video games. Sounds weird I know, a friend of mine (who will mercifully remain nameless) would do the drawings for different stages/parts of the game, and I would write the text. I even wrote a song once (not the music, just lyrics) that I can even remember and laugh about to this day, it was so terrible! Incredibly, I think we even recorded a version of it on cassette tape. It would be so funny to listen to that again, but it has also been taken by the ravages of time (and the fact that I don't keep stuff that I see as junk). As time went on, I wrote short stories and even poetry (both of which I wish I still had). I even had a poem published in my high-school paper, I think that may have been called "Mr. Nobody" (and was rather depressing if I recall). More time passed and when I got to university, I wrote for the student newspaper *The Muse*. I did CD and movie reviews, and I did manage to get a few of them published. I remember even now how thrilled I was to see my name in print and show it to people.

Move ahead even more time (I was doing a degree in English, so I certainly wrote a lot of papers) and my friend had his first novel published (*The Dying Days* by Shannon Patrick Sullivan). It was the first time my name was in print for a long time (I helped him with the editing and got mentioned in the acknowledgements) and I remember distinctly thinking to myself, *I can do more than just be in the acknowledgements, I can have a book published too!* It was the kick in the pants I needed and after a long time (with a huge gap where I did not write) my first novel finally came out in April of 2011 (I had started writing in 2002). Really though, this chapter is not meant to be about my publishing history or writing timeline. It is about how writing makes me feel and it is something I hope that you will try sometime and will hopefully get enjoyment from as well.

As was ingrained in me during my time at university, I always research any topic I write about. So, I did find an article called "The Power of Writing: 3 Types of Therapeutic Writing" (Tartakovsky, 2015.) which really plays into how writing has been beneficial to me. One of the things many of us have done (at some point in our lives) is to keep a journal. For me, I remember being asked to do a journal in school (several times throughout) and I did it until I was around fourteen. Back then I did not think about it much, but I can see clearly now that it was a good outlet, a judgement-free way to pour out your thoughts and feelings. We all have secrets, dark thoughts, or skeletons in our closets, but if you keep a journal (and obviously do not let anyone see it, I have a password on mine) then we are free to explore those thoughts in a healthy way. I recently started keeping a journal again and I am enjoying it. I even use hashtags at the end of each entry, so that way if I ever want to organize it into something, or look back at it, it will be much easier. So, if I wanted to see how I felt about the pandemic, for example, I can just search for a related term. A journal does become a secret (I cannot imagine sharing it, at least not all of it) but a healthy one I can take comfort in and have all to myself. I have read excerpts from journals famous writers have kept—like Ernest Hemingway's—and it makes for a fascinating, if sometimes sad read. As an author, I can hope that someday after I am gone maybe my journal will be published for people to see. Somehow that is comforting and maybe even a little flattering.

With poetry, while I certainly have enjoyed reading it, I have not written many poems (only a few) in the past thirty years. This article does spark my interest and I think it will be time to write one again. Writing poetry will be a good exercise to do in my journal, as then I can go back and see how they improve over time. When you think about music (good music I mean, a lot of what you hear these days is garbage) it is poetry that is made into a song. One of the basic formats for lyrics (though you do not have to do this) is to make words rhyme, you can listen to almost any song and there are words that do that. While I am not a fan, you can hear this in country music often, when words are put together that don't rhyme but are pronounced in a way that seems like they do, they're called slant rhymes. As the article says, poetry can be a way to make sense of memories from our past or discuss something we see in the present. Perhaps we see a person pick up someone's wallet and give it back to them, a kind and generous act however small, this could be a good place to write a poem if you have the time. All of us (well at least ninety percent) have a cell phone so you could send yourself an e-mail (or use the notepad app) that has a poem or at least the start of one. Poems are interesting as well because they can have a certain structure, for example haiku is a kind of poetry of three lines made up of a certain number of syllables per line.

We were on vacation with friends in Ireland in 2019 (back when the world was a lot more normal) and one friend decided we should all write a limerick about Ireland. It was a fun exercise and since I do not intend to do a book of poetry (at least anytime soon), here is what I wrote:

There once were friends from Newfoundland.
They went on a trip to Ireland.
They made merry and drank verily.
Most days they were quite cheerily.
And travelled both there and back again.

Maybe not my best work, but I think it turned out alright. Another interesting writing idea is a letter. You may have heard about this in a movie or TV show; the idea is that you can write to someone who is living or dead, maybe even someone you never met. This letter (which is never supposed to be sent) could reveal some secret you have or at least have some honest feelings that you have not expressed to anyone else. I have found that it feels good to get something that is bothering me off my chest, even if it is only putting it on a computer (or phone) screen. While it may also sound like something from a movie, you could also write to someone who has passed away, a pretend conversation you can have with a loved one. Many times (myself included) we have a loved one die and feel you never said everything you should have, and if you write a letter (again, which will naturally never be sent) you can put those thoughts together and feel you have gotten them out of your mind at least. Of course, this letter (if written sometime after your loved one is gone) could also be a comfort as it will hopefully remind you of the good times you had together.

For me, writing is a way to express my creative side and active imagination. For years I expressed it not by writing novels or short stories (or even the occasional poem) but with role-playing adventures. You might have heard of Dungeons and Dragons, and don't worry if you have not, there is a whole chapter about role-playing for you to enjoy later. When I was a Game Master (and I hope to be again when the whole necessity for isolation finally goes away) I made a lot of effort coming up with characters, story arcs, interesting battles, specific treasures, and generally spent a gigantic amount of time running what is called a campaign. Role-playing is great for anyone interested in writing because it forces you be creative; you exercise your imagination in ways you have not done so before and get immediate feedback from the players (the people who experience your writing). I would ask for feedback, and I was lucky to get it from my friends (for the most part I have only done role-playing with friends, it is usually a better experience). I knew as the years passed that I was getting better as a Game Master, and I think it helped me a lot when it came to writing novels as I had already had experience with crafting together large stories and doing world building. Even just taking a story (they are called adventures in the role-playing world) and making changes or additions to it was great writing practice and something I dearly loved. When I think back on it, I think doing so much with the fantasy genre (which is where Dungeons and Dragons is primarily set) cemented my love for it even more and helped me a lot later when it came to writing short stories. I even found inspiration from role-playing sessions and later wrote three short stories based on characters I played in Dungeons and Dragons and Call of Cthulhu (a horror game). This was a fun way to imagine what my characters did outside of the sessions I played. It was also a chance to have full control and decide what would happen (the Game Master, or Dungeon Master for Dungeons and Dragons does this for role-playing games to a large extent). What the players do in role-playing game does have a large impact on the world or story of course but writing gives you total freedom and it is like you get to play that character whenever you want.

When I first came up with the idea for a novel (*The Newfoundland Vampire* if you are curious) I wrote a little bit—I think the first chapter and a little of the second—but then stopped. The prospect seemed too huge, too daunting a task to write a whole book. So, I get it, I know writing something long like a novel seems impossible but (when I went back to about six years later) I saw the truth; it can be just something you work at over time. I was not in any rush, so as the months went by, I kept writing and eventually, I had a whole book done. I am oversimplifying a little. I did also write an outline (which I would frequently change) of what each chapter would be about, and I was doing research at the time as well. The point is that is you make writing a part of your life (whenever you spend ten minutes or hours every day at it), and you enjoy it, then it becomes a good hobby and maybe if you're lucky, a passion in your life. While my vampire books may just look like a simple fantasy/horror/romance romp (and certainly that is a major part of all four books) they were an important and enjoyable exercise for me.

Like most people, I wonder about different choices I could have made, the road not taken, and that was one of the things I did in my vampire series and short stories. I ended up being a college instructor for a few years, got married, and am now working in the family business. But what if I had made different choices? What if I had never gotten married and met a different woman? What if I had been more successful as an instructor? That was one of the enjoyable parts I found with writing a novel; exploring how I would respond in different situations and image how my life would have turned out with different choices. I made this exercise in imagining easy to do for my vampire books as one of the main characters, Joseph, was heavily based on me. So, every time Joseph was faced with a decision or situation, I could imagine what I would do and have him respond that way. The fascinating part I discovered is that as I got older and some of my ideas changed, I could change some of Joseph's and I could clearly see how different I had become from him. In a lot of ways, I came to see Joseph as a younger and less mature version of myself that had a lot of growing up to do. I did so myself and came to see the world a little differently as I gained experience.

To bring this back to the point, however, I found that writing is a great way to deal with memories, thoughts, and feelings that I had that were never fully resolved. Sometimes, they were things that would kind of itch at the back of my mind from time–to-time. About four years ago I was in a car accident, to be honest it was an accident I caused, and I was lucky that no one was seriously hurt. None the less, it bothered me for months afterwards. It was on my mind especially because it was the last vacation I ever got to go on with my dad (he died a few months later) and I regretted that one of my last memories with him was an unpleasant one. So, time passed, and I decided to write a short story about the accident. I changed names as most authors do when writing about real people, and I think it turned out to be good story. I made it part of a short story collection, and the feelings I had about the accident settled in my mind and I started to move past it. I find that writing about complicated feelings and memories (especially those connected to sickness, hospitals, or death) helps me deal with it. Things that seem messy and complicated in my head are a lot clearer when you put them on paper. After I wrote the short story, I gained perspective on the event. I think more importantly, I learned that no matter what distractions are around you in the car (and there were a few), paying attention is so important when driving, especially in a different country with a rented car. After the chapter was done (and published in *The Chaos Stories: Tales of Magic, Terror, Passion and Blood*) I felt better about the whole experience. I felt like I had dealt with it as much as I could, and it occupied the right spot in my memory.

To give a more recent example, I wrote a chapter on COVID and the whole pandemic as it affected me (Chapter 5). Like lots of people all over the world, the pandemic had a huge impact on my life. When you are in something like a worldwide pandemic it's hard to find perspective. It feels like it might go on for years with no end in sight (and in truth it has been over a year, but the end is now in sight). When I wrote about it, I could see more clearly how lucky I am to be living in Newfoundland where we have only had two lockdowns, only a few deaths, and in comparison, to almost the entire world, really a much easier time. It is one of the stranger events in that I could keep going back to the chapter and change or add things. I could not immediately just put it behind me like a car accident or a death because it is still ongoing. I do recall putting-off writing the COVID chapter until after the first lockdown was finished; the wound was just too fresh to write about when things still seemed so uncertain and hard.

So, while it may seem mundane to write a grocery list, think of it this way; you are organizing your thoughts and making your life better. Why go get groceries twice when you can do it once? If you can see the benefit to that, it is not a big step to see that writing about an experience you had whether it is good, bad, or just ordinary (we all have those moments that stick in our heads) is beneficial. Who knows why your uncle got drunk and embarrassed himself at the staff party? (My uncle did not do this, just an example, of course). Maybe, just maybe though, if you take the time to think about this no-good uncle, you could gain some insight, realize that his behavior is tied to the way he was brought up, or even that alcoholism runs in the family. Writing can be many things; just a fun way to explore your imagination in made-up worlds, a simple journal of events that happened to you during the year, or a deep analysis of an important event that happened to you. That is the great part; you can spend as little or as much time writing as you want. You can scribble it in a notebook or on some post-it, or keep a detailed file saved on your computer. Either way, any activity that makes you feel a connection to your memories or just helps you sort through a shitty day you had at work, will be a benefit to you in the long run. It may sound like work at first, but it is a way to directly connect your thoughts to something physical and an excellent way to help you sort through this wacky, sad, ordinary, boring, and sometimes just plain bizarre thing that is life.

Chapter 2: The Environment

The concept of the destruction of our environment is a large one and sadly, one that a lot of people aren't entirely able to grasp. I can see one of the reasons why, it's part of human nature. We (I am speaking from the North American perspective here) tend to focus on our own lives. The environment gets mixed up in our head with weather a lot (and yes, I know they are related of course), so if it's nice day out we're in a better mood and things like climate change, pollution, garbage and any other number of important issues don't make it into our thoughts. I get it, most people work hard during the week. In their time off they don't want to be fretting about how big their carbon footprint is.

Like a lot of people, I didn't think about the environment when I was young. Hell, I'll even admit that when I was twenty-one it was still only barely registering in my mind. I was fortunate; I was given a car at seventeen and I drove it constantly. A car meant freedom, time to myself, and I took full advantage of it. I was almost always picked up at school and for my senior year in high school I drove back and forth every day and would often come home lunch times as well (I lived close to the school). In my defense, I always did love to walk outside and from the time I was twelve until I was seventeen, I would walk home on any nice day (it was about a twenty-to-twenty-five-minute walk, and I would go through the woods for a lot of it). I have pleasant memories of being outside at school on break time, riding my bike while I listened to music, and just lying on the ground reading comics. Things changed when I was in university. I wanted some independence and when I was twenty-one, I decided to move into the residence at Memorial University. I can see now this was a rather extravagant and silly choice as I only lived about twenty minutes away, but at the time I was convinced it would be a great way to make friends and even get a girlfriend. To return to the point at hand, I noticed that after I ate my breakfast (I did this in my room as I didn't want to have three meals a day at the cafeteria) I would throw out the plastic spoon and bowl. This seems small but it was an important step for me, after doing this for months I knew I had to start caring about the environment, I had to do better.

I started small, looking for biodegradable containers and utensils. I was the one in the group who always wanted to carpool anywhere we went. If it meant picking people up, I would pick them and bring them home. In my university years I was lucky as I had two friends (still have them now) who never drank, and I knew if either of them was going I could always get a run home. When I finished at residence (I only stayed there one semester because I was still a shy person who didn't fit in well socially) I decided to use a carpool service to get back and forth to university.

Yes, I know what you might be thinking, why didn't I ride a bike to university? Well, I think the fact that it was over twenty-four kilometers (mostly uphill) and that I'd be risking life and limb to do so. We are quite behind here in terms of bike lanes (there are almost none!) and in the winter roads are not well plowed, so riding a bike anywhere besides trails is always dangerous. The strange part is that now with university long behind me, I regularly ride twenty-six kilometers or more for pleasure (on a trail of course!). If you lived here in the winter, you'd know that riding your bike for 4-5 months of the year is virtually impossible.

Here is a sobering (and sad) fact: since 1970 (just fifty years ago) half of the ocean's vertebrates have been wiped out. If we don't do better for the environment, coral reefs could no longer exist by 2050. A major car company, Volkswagen, has been cheating on their emissions and have been releasing over forty times the amount of pollution that was legally allowed.

For a more local example there is a mining company called Vale Canada that made a lot of headlines in 2008 for its proposal to use a pond as a place to store toxic waste. This pond is called Sandy Pond and is here in Newfoundland and Labrador, it is sad that while the premiere at the time, Danny Williams, said he would defend the environment he did not stop this development and failed to do so. The crazy part is that according to the federal government companies can turn a pond into a place to store toxic chemicals (and destroy a natural habitat) if they create a habitat of the same size somewhere else! I had to do a fair bit of research and read a long article to discover that despite all the protesting, news articles, and even court cases, Vale Canada still got to use Sandy Pond to store these toxic chemicals and will continue to do so for years to come.

The company has assured the government that when the plant is shut down, they will properly take down all of the structures around Sandy Pond but can they be trusted to do so? I have little faith as was evidence when Argentina base (also here in Newfoundland) was shut down in 1994 leaving behind toxic waste that was never properly cleaned up. The Canadian government (and I am certain many other ones around the world) need to stop prioritizing big businesses, jobs, and profits over the environment! What good will stimulating the economy do when people get sick from contaminated ground water and the environment suffers permanent damage? These are just a couple tiny examples. Sadly, there are millions of abandoned oil wells that all have the potential to spew pollution intro the ground and the air. If you think companies will clean it up, you are sadly mistaken. As oil prices continue to fluctuate more of these companies will go bankrupt, leaving a potential giant environmental disaster to loom over our heads with only a hope and a prayer that some government agency will stop it.

The ocean is more acidic now than it has been in over three-hundred million years! There is plastic waste floating around in the world's oceans that is the size of Texas. I know this is just a collection of numbers and facts, the hard part is making people relate and connect to the environment around us, make them see just what incredible damage we have done in such a short period of time and how we must do better. The immediate problem is that for most people all this environmental damage doesn't (often) have a direct impact on their lives. If you aren't a fisherperson, you don't realize that half of the natural (and farmed) fish stocks in the world are already gone. You have a bad winter with a lot of snow, or you have severe flooding, and it's part of human nature to tend to forget about the bad times and remember the good. Everyone needs to be made keenly aware that the environment is hurting badly, extreme weather (along with lots of other negative climate change effects) is never going to improve unless we see the connection between pollution and climate change.

I've been heavy-handed and mostly negative here, but I can see progress being made, there are some good things. As tough as it is for many people (millions in fact), there is an upside to this whole COVID pandemic. With virtually no cruise ships or planes in the sky, the environment is healing just a tiny bit. Positive changes with the environment have been showing up since the seventies. More and more celebrities are championing causes (and raising money) related to the environment. Leonardo Di Caprio has done a lot of work to raise important environment issues, reduce his charity's carbon footprint and has given plenty of his own money to help. As I've said before (and continue to believe) for better or worse, people listen to celebrities. That's certainly not always a good thing but having any celebrity talk about the importance of saving the environment, it warms my heart a little. Despite all my criticism of the Catholic Church and the Pope, the current Pope Francis is the only one in history to address congress and bring up the importance of saving the environment. The state of California was the first place in the US to completely ban plastic bags. There are cities in the world (including Aspen, Colorado) that now produce all the energy they need with clean energy that is renewable. Once more we see the importance of examples. Hopefully, other cities will be inspired by what can be done with helping the environment.

Even when people are shown the important reasons to protect the environment, they think *what can one person do? What can I do?* You can do a lot. It's not what happens in a single day but over a long span of time that really makes a difference. If people were more aware of the kind of stories of one person truly making a difference, I hope they would start to see the importance of what they can do. Take the simple example of Jaydav Payeng, a farmer in India. When he was just a boy, he decided to make a difference to help the planet, he planted a tree every day. Because of Payeng there is now a forest where there wasn't one before. It is a forest that is full of wildlife and is literally helping us to breath by adding oxygen to the air. He made a tremendous difference and if other people are inspired by him, they can also make a small difference and it will only expand from there. Let's take a simple example let's assume it's not lockdown time and you're a person of the world, going from place to place. In your travels you will see trash, we all do. What if every day you tried to always put one piece of trash in a garbage container? Not only would your actions make our planet cleaner, but it would also be seen by other people and if it made them do the same, or at least reconsider throwing some wrapper on the ground, then it's worth it. Yes, I know this sounds simplistic and even possibly naïve, but it's a start and it's better than doing nothing or making the problem worse. It is encouraging to see that right here in Newfoundland there are volunteers who take time once a year to clean up a section of highway (which leads to the dump and is often full of litter.) It is encouraging to see this cleanup done year after year, not only by adults but children as well.

    I'll give you a current example of what you can do on vacation. A few months ago (in March of 2020) my wife and I were on holiday in Myrtle Beach (a trip cut short due to COVID-19, I'll get into that in the pandemic chapter) and as soon as I woke up the next morning, I checked out the town's website. I wanted to find out what types of materials they took for recycling, along with when and where it would be picked up. Later that day I bought blue recycling bags and even asked a guy who worked at the apartment complex about recycling (he said they don't recycle but he was wrong). I'll admit this took some work as I couldn't find a recycling bin anywhere in the building. Finally, I went to the beach and found recycling buckets there. While it would have been easy to think *I'm on vacation, screw recycling, I want to relax!* I couldn't do that, and neither should you! The Earth never gets a vacation and I always feel better by recycling everything I can. Let's say you work in an office building, and you notice paper has been thrown out. Why not take it to recycling yourself if you're allowed to do it? I suppose I'm something of an extremist. I remember at university (I was there a long time to get a diploma, a degree, and a masters) I used to go to recycle bins and take paper out because I could print on the other side of them. Was I supposed to do that? Probably not, but it didn't do any harm.

    If you live in a big city with a good public transportation system, you don't need a car. When I visit any kind of city that has a subway or bus system, I use it. Driving in big cities is always hard and I avoid it whenever I can. I'm also in reasonable shape and there are lots of times when I'll walk a long distance (sometimes taking an hour or more) rather than call a taxi. I live in Newfoundland and public transportation is to use a word, pathetic. I'll admit I have been fortunate and have always had a car to drive (not always a new one, I've driven some old clunkers in my time). As years went by (to my early twenties) I always chose a smaller, more fuel-efficient car to drive. After some more time passed, I was finally able to get a hybrid. In my defense, I read that unless your car is leaking fluids or its emissions go way up, you might as well drive your car until its almost worthless. So, I drove one car (a Dodge Neon) for over nine years. In 2014 I finally owned a hybrid and I loved it. I'm aware that a hybrid still burns gas, but it is fuel efficient and can go in electric mode, where it puts out no emissions. It's been proven that something as simple as slowing down your driving speed will help the environment, because you burn less gas and it's something that a car like a hybrid highly encourages you to do. Not only did I enjoy seeing what the best route (and the best driving method) was to be in electric mode the most, it made me a calmer driver and overall person. I just started letting most people pass me. Once you plan, are never in rush, and just relax, driving becomes a more enjoyable experience. Passing everyone on the highway is not only unsafe, but also bad for the environment, and gives you a negative mindset. Unless you're a race car driver, if you love the constant adrenaline rush when you drive, you're most likely driving dangerously. Speed kills and burning excessive amounts of gas kills the planet we live on. Just this year, 2020, I got a plug-in hybrid. This means I can go between forty to fifty kilometers (if I drive slowly) and burn zero gas. I am lucky that I can plug in my car when I go to work and so Monday to Friday, I burn little to no gas. As of now I have driven over 1100 kilometers and have not even burned half a tank of gas. I, of course, wanted to go pure electric but due to lack of infrastructure here in Newfoundland (and the cost of pure electric) I was unable to do it. Hopefully in seven or eight years it will become possible.

    Recent events have shown just how crazy it is for the whole world (with a few notable exceptions) to be so incredibly dependent on fossil fuels. The problem has many layers of course, not only are we literally killing ourselves, but we are also damaging the environment perhaps beyond repair. Governments have made economies so dependent on oil that when the price of it goes down it sends many industries and people into financial troubles. Oil is a limited resource and while we have lots left it's just not sustainable in the long term. Wind, solar, and hydro-electric power sources are all renewable, infinite sources of energy that we need to concentrate on immediately if we want to avoid catastrophic damage to our planet.

    I'll end this section with two people; Doctor David Suzuki, and Donald

H. Trump (sadly still president of the USA as I write this in May of 2020). Suzuki is a brilliant scientist who has won many awards and has been raising awareness of the importance of environmental issues tirelessly since 1979. While he is technically a geneticist and not an expert on the environment, his passion and devotion to environmental causes has given him worldwide recognition. I was lucky enough to see him give a speech here in Newfoundland a few years ago. He is an incredible speaker, and I can honestly say it's because of him that I care more about the environment now than I did even five years ago. Aside from all his speeches, books, and documentaries, he is also directly responsible for saving a community in British Columbia from environmental disaster and is considered a hero with many Indigenous Canadians. His message is clear; governments are so obsessed with things like the economy that they have lost sight of the terrible damage being done to our planet, damage that will continue to make people suffer, kill animals by the thousands, and ultimately make our planet less livable as floods, droughts, hurricanes, and erosion of coastal places become more and more frequent.

Of course, I can't finish this chapter without talking about Trump. His administration has done all sorts of terrible things which have done tremendous damage to the environment. He has changed policies that Obama put in place for clean water and air, he claims this is to stimulate the economy but really, he is just obsessed with undoing whatever he can from the previous administration. He pulled the US out of the Paris climate agreement (one of the few countries to do so), spent money to try and stimulate coal production (I wish I was making that up!), he wants to turn two national moments into drilling sites and increase logging activities on public land. He is basically ignoring any reasonable course of action when it comes to the environment and is instead pushing us ever closer to a point where the damage will be beyond repair and generations to come will suffer.

Despite what I just said about Trump, I do believe there's hope. The recent surge in popularity of the electric car, the development of wind and solar power, along with most people trying to reduce, reuse, and recycle where they can. All you can do is lead by example and I'm proud to drive a hybrid car, recycle as much as possible, and always throw out any trash in the proper places. I'm also the kind of guy that will try to encourage others to lead more environmentally friendly lives. Carpool to work, keep your discarded food for compost, try meatless Monday (or even become vegetarian, I'll talk much more about that in another chapter). If you live in a big city, use public transportation or even walk or ride a bike to work. Even just walking a few flights of stairs rather than taking the elevator is something that can help (and will help you be healthier!). We all live on this big blue ball together and if we all just care a little more then we'll all benefit, and future generations will be forever grateful.

Chapter 3: Conventions

I miss going to conventions. I think that it is just one of the things that the pandemic has taken away from everyone. I say that not just as someone who loves to attend them, but also as an author. I have had tables at numerous conventions all over Newfoundland and Labrador (and one in Nova Scotia) and I have done panels at numerous conventions as well. It is true that you often do not appreciate something until it is gone, and such has been the case for me. On a more positive note, the lack of conventions this past year–and-a-half is certainly giving me time to reflect on what conventions mean to me and I have been able to reminisce about all the great experiences I have had at them. For those who do not know, a convention is a celebration of a genre, topic, TV show, movie, hobby, interest, or business. Most of the conventions I have been to have been a celebration of either sci-fi, fantasy, or comic books. I have also gone to specific *Star Trek* conventions, and events I would not necessarily call conventions but a celebration of one thing (in my case ciders and movies at two different festivals). I have also been to a games fair that was all about board games and role-playing games, this was different and while not a convention, was a gathering of people who all had similar interests. Conventions are a chance to meet people with similar interests, enter contests (perhaps most popular at many conventions is the costume contest), attend panels, meet celebrities, and often pick-up merchandise you may not be able to find anywhere else. You can even get stuff signed by your favorite celebrities who sit on a panel to meet people and sign autographs.

I can remember going to a convention here and it was literally only about five tables spread out around a high-school gym. At first, it seemed a waste of time with no celebrities to meet and little stuff to buy. At this tiny convention, however, I met someone (Ron who was president of the club at the time) who told me about a *Star Trek* society in St. John's. I have always loved *Star Trek* and I quickly followed up and joined the group. I would stay with that group for over fifteen years, eventually becoming the president myself before finally leaving. That is one of the great parts of going to a convention, you can connect with all sorts of people who have interests similar (or the same) as yours and discover a whole new way to enjoy what you are into. When I was in school, I was a geek and did not have a lot of friends. When I started going to conventions and meeting people I did not feel so alone anymore, it was a place where I belonged and felt welcome. As I mentioned before, conventions always have people who are part of clubs. For example, at one of the local ones (I am lucky to live in province that normally has multiple conventions throughout the year) there is a board game group. They have board games happening during the convention all the time and you can just stop in to play a game whenever you feel like it. This board game group also was once the *Star Trek* group I alluded to (once called the USS-Avalon Society) and I still know people who are a part of it.

Conventions have always been a win-win experience for me because they not only combine my love of sci-fi/fantasy/horror/comic books/TV/movies, they also often involve traveling (which I also dearly love) so getting to do both together can really be something magical for me. When I was in my early twenties and still did not have a girlfriend, I had a lot of time on my hands (I suppose I still have a fair bit being married with no children) and wanted to meet new people and indulge in my hobbies. I decided to go to a convention in Dartmouth, Nova Scotia as it would be a chance (and I was correct in assuming my only chance) to meet Majel-Barrett Roddenberry. For those who do not know Majel-Barret was the widow of Gene Roddenberry (who created *Star Trek*) and someone who acted in various shows (playing four different roles) and was something of a legend in the *Star Trek* world. For me, the trip was almost as important as the convention, I had never gone on a trip completely by myself out of the province. Luckily, I keep the important sentimental stuff and I found the old program booklet, it was called the "Maritime Science Fiction Festival" and it happened in April of 1996.

This brings me to one of the most important aspects of a convention, the immediate feelings of friendliness and inclusivity. When I arrived in Dartmouth, I was excited. I have loved *Star Trek* since I was four years old and the chance to meet Majel-Barrett got me down to the convention area of the hotel before it even started. Back then I was more into cosplay (wearing costumes to conventions/movie premieres or other public events) and I was wearing a *Star Trek* uniform, so it was easy to tell I was going to the convention. Within ten minutes of getting off the elevator and wandering around a guy came up and introduced himself. He said he was part of a local sci-fi group and asked if I wanted to come back to his room as no events had started. I know it sounds a little strange reading this but (and I can only speak from the male perspective) there is this feeling of trust at a convention, and I said yes right away. When I went upstairs, they had several rooms (he was there with friends and other people from his group), and he offered me a snack and said I could hang out there, play video games, or just chat with people for a while. I politely declined but it put me in a good mood, made me feel welcome and I had a great time at the convention.

The other big part of conventions is meeting people who are involved with the things you adore. I love lots of geeky things and I enjoy meeting new people at conventions, so it is a win-win for me. I just mentioned Majel-Barrett (and yes it was good to meet her) but I was so shy back then that I only barely spoke to her. As time passed and I went to more conventions I became more outgoing and I got to meet and talk with lots of people, both celebrity and non-celebs alike. The first person I will talk about is a celebrity, albeit an Atlantic Canadian one but he is such a great guy that I wanted to start with Mike McCluskey or his stage name, Fat Apollo (this is not an insult in any way, he loves that name!). Mike is one of funniest and friendliest guys I have ever met. One of the reasons I go to conventions here is for the chance to chat and hang out with him. His story-time panel is something I never miss (unless I have a panel myself) at every convention and he is someone who always made me feel welcome and happy that I came. While you hear lots of great stories at his panel, you get to hear even better (and more interesting) ones if you buy him a drink and hang out at the bar. He has been the Master of Ceremonies for every Atlanti-Con for a reason, he has not only the gift of gab but the ability to talk with any celebrity and make them also feel welcome.

When you go to enough conventions you get what I will call con-friends, these are people you are friends with but only see them when you are at a convention (and yes like anything in life there are a few exceptions to this of course). Mike is certainly a con-friend and I heartily look forward to seeing him again when conventions can resume. With conventions it is not just the guests you meet but the people who run the conventions as well. Atlanti-Con is a sci-fi/fantasy/comics/gaming and anime convention held in Corner Brook (on the west coast of Newfoundland). I love the west coast of the province and I love this convention; I believe I have attended all but one of them and I have missed it the past two years. This is a convention where I am not an attendee but rather an author/guest and as such I get to experience it in a different way that most people do. I remember getting to Atlanti-Con one year and I knew from the first hour or so it would be a great time. One of the volunteers immediately came to help me (opened the door, helped me with my hand cart, those kinds of things) and it made me feel so welcome. Atlanti-Con is a smaller convention and as such you get to know everyone involved. The main person of course was Jeff Keeping (as I write this Jeff has decided to step back from the convention but as I am talking about the past, I will leave it at that). Jeff always did a wonderful job running the convention and always came around to talk with every vendor/guest/author to see how they were doing each day. Jeff listened to suggestions I had regarding food (which might sound small but as a vegetarian I really appreciated it) and any other aspects which may need improvement. He grew Atlanti-con so that it went from a hotel to the university (Memorial has a small campus in Corner Brook) to the biggest building in the city, the Pepsi Center, all within five years. Atlanti-Con was the first convention where I got to be an invited guest and it will always hold a dear place in my heart. I will also say that some of the best experiences I have ever had both in terms of parties, hanging out with the guests, and selling my books all have come from being at Alanti-Con. It is my favorite convention, and I cannot wait to be able to go back there. When you go to a convention you are probably only there for a few hours, you see some celebs, maybe get some stuff signed, attend a few panels, possibly buy some stuff, and go home. A convention for an author with a table (as I was) is a whole different kettle of fish. For Altanti-Con (and other conventions) I am there usually from the moment the convention starts, to the moment it ends, and I spend a great deal of that at my table selling my books and other wares. Sure, I can take breaks any time I want, and I usually have one or more panels I run but still for most of two days, I am there in one spot. Don't get me wrong, this is not a bad thing, I get time to write, to think, chat with the people around me, talk with people who visit my table, admire the costumes, but still, like anything after five or six hours, it can be a grind. One of the things I have discovered that makes the time pass much quicker is to make friends with people at the tables around you (as much as they want to, of course). I was at Hal-Con in 2013 (sci-fi/fantasy/anime convention in Halifax, Nova Scotia) and as with any convention, I had some down time where it was just me at my table. I had been there for the whole day and luckily the woman next to me (whose husband was an artist and was selling his art) was friendly and struck up a conversation. We talked for a good hour or more that day about lots of different things and it made the whole convention a more memorable and enjoyable experience.

   Returning to Atlanti-Con, I also had several great chats with a guest one year (also in 2013, it was a great year for me and conventions). When I go to Atlanti-Con I stay at the Glynmill Inn, which is where all the other guests stay. As a consequence, I am bound to run into them (also Jeff always plans some kind of get together after the convention both Saturday and Sunday which I am invited to) and such was the case with Gary Jones. If you do not know who Gary is, I understand, he was on the show *Stargate SG-1* and I know that because I am a geek who loves sci-fi shows (Gary has a great sense of humor and knows all this). So, we ended up having breakfast together twice and had a great chat at a bar where he and the other guests ended up Saturday night. Gary is one of the nicest people I have ever talked to, and he really tries to get to know you. I admitted to him early on that I was never a fan of *Stargate SG-1* and he was good with that, which shows a level of maturity I appreciated. While it is fun to talk with a guest at a convention, seeing them in a more relaxed atmosphere where they loosen up, maybe have a few drinks, is a whole other experience. That night in 2013 at the Grenfell campus university bar was one of the best conventions experiences I had, and it was just about having fun, not being impressed with a celebrity and connecting with people. This is the kind of fun you can have if you go to a convention, not only the chance to meet someone from a show or movie you enjoy but also to hang out with them and other people all with the same interests as you. If you are shy person who has trouble meeting people and going to social events, a convention is a great way to get out of that rut, as much as you feel comfortable doing, in a relaxed atmosphere.

   They say not to meet your heroes, but I firmly disagree. I have met lots of people I looked up too and admired (yes some were heroes of the geek world to me) and I have always enjoyed the experience. I have already discussed Majel-Barrett (though she was certainly a hero) so I will talk about some of other celebs that meant a lot to me. Not to get too heavy, but as you get older people die, people you knew, celebs and people close to you (I talk about the death of my dad in Chapter 15). I got to meet several celebrities before they died, and they were all unique and enjoyable experiences. The biggest one (that I think most people would know) is Stan Lee. I was in Florida on holiday with my wife and parents and was lucky to have a convention only a few hours away I could attend. There were other people there (including Wil Wheaton and Karl Urban, great guys I enjoyed talking to a lot) but the main draw for me was Stan Lee. In case you do not know, Stan Lee was the co-creator of many famous comic book characters such as *Spiderman, X-Men, Fantastic Four, Hulk, Daredevil, Iron Man, Black Panther, Ant-Man, Doctor Strange* and others. He was also the owner of Marvel Comics for many years, their spokesperson, and had many cameos in Marvel movies. Suffice it to say he changed comic books forever and helped make the many Marvel movies and TV shows the smash hits (and even Oscar winners) they are today. I have loved comic books since I was ten years old with The Hulk and Spiderman being two of my favorite characters. Suffice it to say I was excited to meet their creator. I stood in line for about two hours, spent a good deal of money (over three-hundred dollars) and finally had the chance to meet Stan and get him to sign my *Hulk* t-shirt. I thanked him for all the years of pleasure he has given me from his characters, and he smiled and said, "thank you for being a fan all these years and you're welcome." It was a quick moment with lots of people behind me in line, but I will never forget it and I now have the shirt in a frame on my wall. The other person I will never forget meeting is possibly someone you have never heard of; René Auberjonois who played the character Odo from *Star Trek: Deep Space Nine*. I used to be a lonely person, I think it goes back to how much I hated high school and felt like an outcast, and when I watched René play Odo I could relate (his character also talked a lot about loneliness and not belonging in early seasons of the show). I loved *Star Trek: Deep Space Nine* and I always hoped that one day I would get to meet René and tell him that I thought he was a great actor and that his portrayal of Odo helped me get through a difficult time in my life. I got that chance at Avalon Expo in 2017 and he was a warm, gracious person who despite the difficulties at the convention was friendly and pleasant to everyone there wish I had gotten him to sign something, but I did get a few nice photos and a memory I can hold onto forever. It is worth noting, however, that René was quite outspoken on Twitter during Avalon Expo and he said some negative things. While he had every right to be angry it was a tad unprofessional what he said online and could have hurt the future of Avalon Expo (and hurt the vendors who were there.) Back then I used Twitter a lot more and responded to some of his tweets, he was reasonably upset about what happened at the convention but not at the vendors, fans and other people involved, which was understandable. Of course, it is not just about meeting celebs, I have been lucky to meet not one but two local artists who I later got to do covers for three of my vampire books (and the cover for this book). I met my current editor at a convention (who is also an author herself), she is one who helped make this book even better. I even had the unique pleasure of not only meeting someone who created games I love, Steve Jackson, but playing and beating him at a game of *Munchkin* at a convention in Ireland.

Conventions are a lot like life, they are full of good people, fun events, surprises, and sadly of course a few ugly parts and disappointments. I know that there have been women who have been treated poorly at conventions by men. This is often due to what is called gatekeeping (which just means being a jerk and not letting someone else enjoy the same hobby you do just because they do not have the same breath of knowledge you do), and of course there has been some improper behavior with women in costumes. It is a simple thing when you consider it, you would not just randomly take a picture of a stranger because she is attractive or wearing a costume in a regular setting (that is weird and creepy), so why do it at a convention? It has taken a while, but I think men are finally getting the message that just because a woman looks sexy/amazing/beautiful in a costume (or a man of course) does not give you the right to harass them or take their picture without their permission. People who cosplay at conventions put a lot of time and effort into their costumes. They want people to enjoy it and compliment them, all you need to do is ask their permission before you take the shot. Besides, why get some blurry/crappy picture of someone walking by in a great costume when they will happily pose for you, and you get a great pic? It is a no-brainer, do not be a dick in regular life and the same goes for a convention.

I will also say that everyone likes to be the center of attention sometimes, everyone likes a compliment. I have been lucky enough to have had lots of moments where someone will come to a panel I have done at a convention (I usually do one on writing and publishing, but I have also done one on speaking Klingon) and be really into it. Having a stranger (or someone you know) come up to you afterwards and say they loved your panel, you have encouraged them to write and ask you questions is a wonderful feeling, it makes your whole day. I have also been lucky to have the same happen when I was at a table about my books. Once about a year after my first book came out (and I had been in the paper twice and on the radio twice) two young women came up to me gushing about how much they enjoyed my book. This was at *Sci-Fi on the Rock*, Newfoundland and Labrador's longest running and most successful convention. They even asked to have their pictures taken with me! It was a shining moment in my life that may sound small but meant so much. Most of the time as an author I just write by myself, spend a huge amount of time editing and planning a book, finally put it out and then wait for any kind of feedback on it. While I enjoy the positive comments more, I admire anyone who comes up to me at a convention to share their thoughts on one of my books (good, bad, or somewhere in between). If you hated my books, come up and tell me why, I promise you I can take it, I would only ask you try to come up with ways I could improve my writing rather than just spew negativity.

    Conventions are a way to express the joy you have for a hobby/passion/interest with others in a fun way. They show you that you are not alone in your love of whatever you are into. What greater thrill could there be than reading a book, loving it and then getting the chance to meet the author? As someone who has met George R. R. Martin (who wrote *Game of Thrones*) I can tell you it is sublime and unique experience that you need to experience someday if you can. Conventions remind you of what life can be like, people being friendly with each other, having fun, doing things they love and welcoming guests who come from far away. Mike, Fat Apollo, has come here for many years because he loves the conventions but more important because he loves Newfoundland and Labrador and the people who live here. If a convention can make someone feel happy and welcome, then it is making that person's life a little better. A convention is (and should always be) about spreading joy and celebrating that hobby that you love so much. It is a chance to meet people who have portrayed (or write about) the characters you love. It is a chance for local artists to shine and offer you someone unique to buy that you could not buy in a store or online. Conventions are an opportunity for you to see that there are people and groups you can connect with locally and hopefully make a few new friends. More than anything conventions are (almost always) a place you can feel happy and accepted, perhaps more so than you have felt in a long time. They are a world onto themselves and a place I cannot wait for go back to when it is safe and possible for us all to meet again.

Chapter 4: Children

I'll start this off with some brutal honesty. I don't have children and a part of me doesn't even like children (at least not enough to have my own). I've had arguments where I've been told that my reasoning is insane because it means I'm anti-life, but as I did then, I'll clarify it now. What I really mean is that I'm certain that some (read millions) of people will have children no matter what I say or do. So, humanity is not going to die out for lack of a gene pool. What I mean is that I believe that there are plenty of people who have children that really should not (or at least have too many) and everyone should seriously consider not having children (if you do not already) or perhaps just stop with one. One of the biggest reasons for that is overpopulation. We have strained the resources and the environment of this planet to the breaking point with too many people. There was even a recent study that found sixty percent of American adults are concerned about having children due to the carbon footprint it will create. When you think about it about ninety-nine percent of problems are caused by people, so if we had less of them then the world would be a happier place. For a whole host of reasons, I think that at least a tenth of the people who have children become terrible parents and therefore make the world a worse place.

I have extreme points of view and I'm stubborn—once my mind is made up, it's almost impossible to change it. I suppose for me it comes down to the experiences I had with children, (including when I was one) and the bad quickly outweighed the good. I was a serious child from early on. For me, time to myself became important I'd say from the age of ten onwards, and my tolerance for silly, immature, annoying behaviour had already begun to decrease. I longed to be grown-up not only for freedom but to get away from other children that bothered me to no end. Yes, I did the usual childhood things of playing with action figures, playing ice hockey (I only did this once, I was never into sports). Playing in the snow and making tunnels, getting on dirt bikes, doing make-believe and dress-up; all that stuff. I remember that things started to change for me when I realized that I just didn't like the way children acted (even though I was one myself). I think I was around eleven or twelve and I was in swimming lessons. I had gotten far (I loved to swim, still do but I hate public pools) and we were learning about what to do if a canoe overturned. The instructor got us to swim up underneath an overturned dingy and taught us how you could just hang onto it if you had to in the ocean. Then he left and swam away to let us see what it would be like. All the other children started to scream (I guess because it was unexpected) but I just calmly treaded water and waited for him to return. I could swim and I knew I could get out of there, so why did all the other kids have to be so immature? I suppose the only answer is that I was never a typical child and the other children I spent time with (at least outside of my friends) were and as such I always felt out of place and perplexed by them.

I'm the kind of person where if there's a screaming child in a store I will leave and wait in the car. A child screaming/acting out or a baby screaming are for me two of the worst sounds in the world and I made sure I would never have to deal with them on any kind of regular basis. I had conversation at work a few weeks ago and one of our older staff members (over 60 years old) talked about how while she loves her grandchildren, sometimes they really wear her out. She went on to describe how their behaviour was just terrible on this evening when she was babysitting, I was there and felt I had to join in. I talked about how I never regretted not having children and how I was glad I would never have to deal with a grandchild. My nights are (most often) filled with peace and quiet, my time is my own and I only deal with adults who can (usually) be dealt in rational ways. I was expecting someone to say that I made a selfish choice, and I just did not know what I was missing but no one did. In fact, another woman (who has a teenage son) spoke up and said she thought it was great that I was so certain about what I wanted and did not want in life. We agreed that many people have children due to family/society/friend or spousal pressure (and of course the save a marriage reason, which is nonsense.) "The belief that having children will improve one's marriage is a consistent myth "(Johnson, 2016). If you read the article, you discover the exact opposite is true, having children puts strain on a marriage. Therefore, if you have trouble with your marriage, see a counselor, having children will (most likely) only make your problems worse. While I know I perhaps could have been a good father, I chose not to and most days I am happy with that choice.

An article I read (mainly just a large list of questions) is, I'm aware, meant to be amusing and satirical but Joshi still presents valid reasons for not having children. I've always been aware of the passage of time and by that, I mean I've always valued my free time highly. Think about it, if time to yourself is free that means times you spent doing something else (like your job) is in some sense paid time. It's the idea that I'm doing something I don't like, so there must be some payment involved to get me to do it. If you love your job, you are one of the lucky ones and I am a little jealous but still in the minority, so my argument holds up (Jones, 2020). Why subject yourself to something unnecessarily when you don't even enjoy it? Yes, I know everyone (virtually) has to work to earn a living and everyone does have to do some number of chores to live in any kind of domicile, it seems that young children is like committing to work at something where you will lose all this time away from something else you would rather be doing. I know that when children grow up that life can be a lot different. Children can help with chores, you can play board games with children, video games, go to movies, ride bikes. I think for me I just never wanted to put in the time and effort to get to that point. Do I have regrets? I will admit there are fleeting moments (not often, perhaps two or three times a year) where I wonder what it would be like to have children. I think about how I could have an adult son or daughter by now and how different my life would be. Ultimately, however, I believe life is about pluses and minuses, for me I always felt having any children was too big a sacrifice and I am happy with the choice I made.

    Can every parent honestly say they enjoy getting up in the middle of the night to deal with a crying baby? They enjoy being exhausted for days (or months) on end because of a colicky child? They would say no they don't enjoy it but it the end it's all worth it. This is where I really start to diverge from people who think that way; it's not worth it for me. Life is hard enough, you work, you're tired, you deal with all the pressures in life of bills, upkeep on your place, taxes, elections, getting older, bad weather, relatives you don't like, holidays, weddings, funerals, sickness and then you decide, you know what? Life isn't nearly challenging enough. I need to put a strain on my relationship and make my life way harder (for possibly ten years or more) and have children which I am in no way obligated to do. Does that make any sense? Certainly not to me.

This is a male point of view and while I'm the one writing this book, I can at least reference an article written by a woman about this topic. I read an excellent article in *The Atlantic* which discussed all the reasons why women choose not to have children. Some women (much more so than men) are told that their lives are not complete if they do not become a mother (Gilbert, 2015). Most women are told that without a child to nurture they will not be using some essential part of their psyche and are also pressured as their parents age to provide them with grandchildren. All the notions and pressures by society (and family) that women are subjected to are of course irrational and often false. It is also interesting to note that the more educated a woman is, the less likely she is to have children. The stats speak for themselves; in the 1970s about one in ten women didn't have children, by 2015 that was one in five and for women with college degrees it's one in four. While I could not find any stats for Canada, it is most interesting that "A quarter of educated American women are getting through life without ever having children." (Gilbert, 2015). While I am sure Canada may be a little different, I think it is a trend that women are having less children now than they did in the 1970s.

If you take emotion out of the equation and think about having children rationally, the drawbacks just outweigh the advantages (at least for a lot of people). We've all heard the argument that not having children is selfish and I'm sure for some people that's the case. As I've stated earlier, however, one of the major (I'd argue perhaps the biggest) issue the world is facing is overpopulation. When you choose to have a child (or more than one) you are putting a greater strain on the planet and may in fact be making life worse for your children rather than better. The notion that having a child is the most worthy and noble thing a woman can do is simply an outdated, false notion that has been impressed upon women by society. As someone who studied Philosophy, I would say that the most noble and purest thing anyone can do is to become the best version of themselves and find some way to make the world better. Having a family is not a requirement for either of those things.

Some people say not having children is selfish, but I'd argue it's quite the opposite. When I get old (which is different for every person, but for me I think it will be when I'm in my eighties) I'm not expecting a child to sacrifice months or years of their life to look after me. I hope my wife will be around to help but if neither of us can manage, we'll get a nurse or go into a seniors' home or just do something else. I won't be a burden or obligation to a child because we didn't have one. People should be free to lead their own lives, and having children (often I'll admit, not always) means that someone will have to look after an elderly/sick parent at some time in their life. I'll never subject a child to watching me get sick and die, and I think this is unselfish as it can be truly a horrendous experience. I can tell that watching my own father die was a terrible experience that seemed to go on forever (in truth it lasted about five weeks) and took me a long time to get over it.

I'll bring in some more personal examples (without mentioning names of course). I don't have a huge number of friends, but I think an interesting pattern has emerged among the couples I know. I have other friends (and relatives) who are married (several of them longer than me) who do not have children and are happily married. Of the couples I know, three of them who have children got divorced, nine couples who did not have children (eight of them including us are still together) and four other couples who had children are still together. I know this does not prove anything in terms of statistics but most of my friends (and some family) either did not have children or got divorced after having them. The pattern here with children and my friends certainly has shaped my personal view towards them and influenced my decision not to have any.

As you may have gathered, I have a small family and one of our Christmas parties is now down to six people. I don't think that's sad, it's just what happens in life. I even know one couple who choose to adopt children (granted because they couldn't have any) which is, I'll admit, an extremely selfless and noble thing to do. For a long time, parties were clearly divided in our circle of friends, we would have parties and have to clearly state not to bring children, as they are adult parties. I remember being at a staff party (when I used to be an instructor) and someone just brought a child along. I found it off-putting and strange in an environment where people were drinking and cursing. Is this an event you want to bring your child to?

Once my wife planned a girls' weekend thinking that it would be obvious for her friends to not bring any children, but nope! A friend decided it would be fine to bring her five-year-old child because she couldn't find a babysitter. Suffice it to say it ruined her weekend. Yes, I can hear you asking, "How miserable can you be?" I'm not miserable at all. We have a foster child in the Dominican Republic, we support charities when we can (both local and not), I do my best to help people in need, and I'm certainly friendly to anyone's child. I have had some lovely times with my niece and nephew but none of that means I want children.

Let's look at this from an entirely scientific/mathematical point of view. There are way too many people on this planet. If you don't believe it just look at any kind of video of Tokyo, Mexico City, Los Angeles, or any other major populated city. We are using up are resources at a non-sustainable rate, the pollution we create is out of control, the oceans are filling up with garbage, just here in North America we throw out enough food to feed the rest of the world. Think about that! One continent's food waste is enough to feed everyone else on the planet! It's disgusting and wrong but there is a solution that can help; lower birth rates all over the world. There is a movement called zero population growth which I'm fully on board with. The idea is that birth rates need to match up with immigration patterns (in and out of countries) and the rate of deaths. We already have too many people on earth. To put it in current perspective (and once again sounding a little harsh) human beings are like a virus on this planet. We have consistently destroyed and depleted everything on the Earth. If there were less (or at least a stable number of us) it would give the Earth a chance to recover. It's important to note here that this idea (and my thoughts) is not for people to stop having children, obviously that doesn't work. If fewer couples had children (or at least less) then the population would eventually reach a steady rate where the number of births approaches the number of deaths each year. I am also of the belief that health clinics (and whatever other organization can) giving out birth control to teenagers/underprivileged/high risk groups, then this could also help stabilize the population. I'm happy to know that by not having children I have helped make the world a little easier for future generations.

Were there moments that I had doubts? Yes of course, everyone has doubts. When it came time for me to get a vasectomy (because I was tired of birth control and the small worry that happened every month) there were enough doubts that I cancelled it the first time. It took a couple more years and a lot of thinking before I was completely certain and went ahead with it. I think it takes a long time to really get to know yourself and I was in my mid-thirties before I really knew what I wanted and what I didn't. For me life is about my wife, my hobbies, writing of course, friends, family, travel, time to myself, exercise and freedom to do what I want.

Like most people I get home from work, and I have a few hours to myself. I get more time to relax on the weekends and we go on vacations (I even occasionally go on trips without my wife). But I always find there's never enough time to do the things I want to do. One of the biggest struggles I think most of us face is how to use the time we have well, to be productive, and to feel good about ourselves and what we've accomplished. Having a child (or children) is just not what I see as a valuable use of my time. I want to spend my retirement years traveling, relaxing, and doing all the things I never got a chance to do enough of. So, in the end if you're certain you want a child then have one, but take your time and think about it carefully. Is it what you really want, are you prepared to make all the sacrifices needed, especially for the first few years with a small child? If you think about it rationally (not just emotionally) and decide to have children, then I support your choice fully. I think the major issue the world is facing is that many people don't consider it long and hard enough when it comes to having children. We are all unique and I think the most important thing you can do is decide what will truly make you happy and do it. For me that meant not having children and I am asking you (if you are in the position) to consider if this is the same for you. The world is an overcrowded place, and I am content that when I am gone, there will be just a tiny bit more space available on the planet for someone else.

Chapter 5: COVID and the Pandemic

You would think that in 100 years we would have learned something, been prepared to deal with it, but sadly the answer for a lot of the world (certainly the US) is no. The COVID-19 pandemic hit the world hard in March of 2020 and as I write this (in June of 2021) we are only just starting to see the light at the end of the tunnel. Governments (including parts of the US) did a terrible job in response to the pandemic and caused needless suffering and hardship to millions of people. The death toll for the world due to COVID-19 stands at over three million, notably over 580,000 of them in the US (Worldometer, 2021). Right here where I live (Newfoundland, Canada) we have had just 7 deaths (Government of Newfoundland and Labrador, 2021) and it is hard to grasp mentally how large three million deaths are in comparison, it is certainly one of the worst tragedies that the world has faced in over sixty years. To be honest it is hard for me to even grasp the number of US deaths. We have less people in Newfoundland Labrador than that, so it would be like virtually everyone I ever knew was gone and our huge province (geographically speaking) was empty.

This chapter is going to be dark and depressing; it is just the nature of it but it's important to discuss. I will, however, try to show the positive side for me personally and how the world at large can become better when this terrible pandemic is behind us. It is already incredible how in just a few months terms like *social distancing*, *household bubble* and *community spread* have become commonly used and their meanings known to all. When you left someone's house or sent an e-mail, you used to get closing remarks like 'take care', 'drive safe' or 'have a good weekend' but increasingly it's 'stay safe' or 'keep well.' It is also incredible how something you commonly here all the time is "15 cases today, not good!" or something similar. I often do deliveries for work, and I have shown up at salons and discovered people will not even say hello, they will just state the number of cases we had today. It is a bizarre (and I think rather pointless) phenomenon I will be glad to see come to an end. Unless you are completely out of touch you know how many cases as it is almost impossible to avoid. I will also state that I'm in no way making light of this worldwide tragedy or trying to say I had it harder or easier than other people. All I can do is talk about how the pandemic affected me (and the people close to me) and explore my thoughts and feelings on it. For anyone who has contracted COVID-19 and/or had someone they know die from it, I am deeply sorry and hope this chapter gives you a little comfort in seeing it from my perspective.

Let us start at the beginning (at least for me). Like most people, I started to hear about COVID-19 in January of 2020, when it started in Wuhan, China. Then it was called the Corona virus or the derogatory Wuhan Virus. I don't tend to panic; it was in China which is a long way from Newfoundland, and I honestly thought that in a few months it would go away. Remember the flesh-eating bacteria and H1N1? There was lots of talk when these viruses were active that it would get bad, become worldwide and kill millions. While H1N1 and the flesh-eating bacteria did cause some deaths it certainly did not go worldwide. I thought it would be the same for Corona. I was wrong.

One of our staff at O'Keefe Agencies, who I will call Ronald, talked about it a lot and how bad it will get, and I'll admit that in this case he was right. My wife and I had planned a trip to Myrtle Beach, South Carolina (our first time going there) and while we had some concerns, we simply took extra precautions and went. We brought medical grade wipes, gloves, and plenty of sanitizer, cleaned all around our seats on the plane (we had several flights to get there and back) and felt alright about going there. The first week or so we were there everything was fine. Sure, I noticed that groceries stores were out of stuff like toilet paper, wipes and paper towels but I just thought it was people panicking (and I was mostly right). Less than a week later, March 12, everything changed. My Mom and brother were calling and texting about how concerned they were. My father-in-law started calling about rumors of Canada closing the border to travel, and my sister-in-law was sending me links from CNN and other news sources.

The next day, which was indeed a Friday the 13th, the Prime Minster of Canada (Justin Trudeau) talked about possibly closing the border and suggested all Canadians who were outside the country to come home as soon as possible. Personally, all the pressure and the constant disturbing news reports on the Internet was doing a number on my stomach and I found it hard to relax or sleep. I listened to a podcast (and read it on a local news site, VOCM) that the pandemic was a good time to cut back on social media, and so I did. For first time in my life, I just stopped checking

Facebook. I found that all Facebook was doing was to make me more anxious and upset about the developing pandemic. Any news that was critical to me I'd see on VOCM, or my wife would tell me, so for about three weeks I didn't use Facebook and that did help a little.

On March 13th, we decided we had to leave Myrtle Beach almost two weeks early and get home. We booked tickets on the earliest flight we could get and spent our last days there enjoying the sun, warm temperatures, and friendly people. Then we were home in Newfoundland on March 17th, to begin our two-week isolation (which at that point was only suggested by government and not a requirement). The COVID-19 pandemic has been hard on most people (I would say ninety percent or more) and for me it was worrying even more so because I had been a mild germaphobe for a good twenty years and had always hating getting sick, germs, hospitals, and disease but now I had a reason to be really worried There was a movie (that was quite good but scared the crap out of me) called *Contagion* that is an accurate representation of what a pandemic looks like. Of course, when I saw the movie back in 2011, I didn't think I'd ever see one. Like most people I figured it was something that happened a long time ago and I would never have to deal with it, once again I was wrong. Most of the time, I do not think about the government, our rights and freedoms, or our travel and border policies. I'm lucky as they do not usually matter to me but suddenly, they did. It is easy to forget the kind of power and control the government can impose on a regular citizen but during the pandemic it became crystal clear.

I have been visiting the US my whole life and I had rarely felt uncomfortable there, but in March of 2020 it was different. I had the real fear that if Canada did close the border to the US, I'd be faced with the problem of how I would get home. I do have friends and relatives in the US, but how much could I have really depended on them? If the border was closed for months and I was stuck in the US, I wondered how I would cope. In Canada (and lots of other countries) you have freedom, like the ability to move around and visit other places. During an emergency (such as a pandemic) a freedom such as travel can be suspended or even stopped completely. It was something I never thought I'd have to deal with but as 2020 would show me, I would have to deal with a great many new and unknown things.

I know that millions of good people in the US are doing everything they can to help; they know masks are needed, they practice social distancing and stay home whenever possible. The people I think are much more to blame for the current pandemic state in the United States are those in charge. I think the fact that Trump was impeached not once but twice (only US President in history to ever have that happen) gives a clear indication of what kind of leader he is. As we are talking about the pandemic, however, I will say "the federal coronavirus response shows a president dead set on avoiding responsibility for the pandemic" (Peters, 2020). It is heartbreaking to think that over half a million people have died in the US and this number could have been much lower if a proper response was made. (For the sake of clarity, it is worth noting that I wrote some of this chapter in 2020 and obviously feel differently about President Biden). The governors and mayors who ignored common sense, medical officials, and scientists so they could open stores, let people back on beaches, and a whole host of other things that were done way to soon did their constituents wrong. The governor of Florida, Ron Desantis', (a republican of course) response to the pandemic "has been a disaster" (Alvarez, 2020). I wish I were kidding about the governor of Florida who declared wrestling to be an essential service. For now, I'd like to talk about a good article I found on how COVID-19 is like going through the five stages of grief for a loved one, except it's a shared experience for the whole world. In case you are not aware, the stages of grief are denial, anger, bargaining, despair and acceptance. You can read about it yourself with this interesting article by Robert Weiss called "COVID-19 and the Grief Process. What happens to our differences when our experience is shared?"

Denial is a powerful notion and like a lot of people, I thought the corona virus would be like other ones over the past ten or so years, H1N1, flesh eating virus and bird flu. I'm not making light of any of these viruses, I know that people died, and it was serious. My point is that other viruses like bird flu did not cause the whole world to grind to a halt and kill almost a million people. I thought that the corona virus would be bad for a while, some people would die but being isolated in Newfoundland, life would continue the same as normal. I was wrong. I exercise, get plenty of sleep, and eat healthy and I've always been careful with hand washing, hand sanitizer, and not touching public surfaces. As such (with I'm sure some luck and genetics thrown in) I've never been seriously ill. The worst I ever had was chicken pox in high school and as I write this, I haven't even had a cold in over two years. All that said, I guess I did have some denial in thinking I couldn't get Corona virus (I didn't then, but I know it was possible), at least before we flew home. Flying down in early March to South Carolina it was mostly the same; a few people wore masks and cleaned around their plane seats as we did but going back was a lot different. Airports were busy and a lot more people were wearing masks, people looked at each other nervously and you could feel tension in the air. I was sitting in a Toronto airport waiting to get on a flight home, and an older woman next to me was coughing. By then the pandemic was on the news nonstop and it entered my head that she could have the virus and that I might have just contracted it. I was mildly relieved when she said, "I don't have it, I just have a lung condition." It was nice of her to offer this as I was probably just one of several people concerned with a woman coughing. I thanked her and tried to think of something else, but it was hard. My denial was gone with fear and anxiety taking root in the back of mind. It would die down in the months to come but ultimately it just became something you must live with as we all get used to what is being called the 'new normal'. The scary part of COVID-19 is that there are at least fourteen different strains, all varying in severity and that even if you get a strain that doesn't kill you, it can still have negative long-lasting (and permanent) effects on your health. I know deep down I could get it and all I can do is be careful and practice good hygiene.

 The next stage is anger. When a loved one dies you are angry for a whole host of reasons, like the way the person died. You might be angry that it was so soon, mad because now you are left with more responsibility (including potentially an elderly parent or children that need care). For the pandemic of course it meant something totally different. Many people (not me) were angry at China and even went so far as to claim they released the virus on purpose. I will say that while it was strongly recommended that I stay home from work, I just couldn't do that. My brother, Mom, and I own a small business and to shut it down completely for any long period would be a huge financial blow for us. I know what you're thinking, I'll explain. We immediately switched to curb-side pickup, with no customers allowed in the store. When bringing orders out to cars I wore a mask and gloves and never got within six feet of anyone. I washed my hands till they bled some days and went through more pairs of disposable gloves than I can count. I listened to what the government told me and did not have any social events until we were at a lower pandemic level (in Canada we had a level system, five being the highest with the most restrictions, and one being the lowest. As I write this, we are at level two). The fact that I followed the rules does not mean I wasn't angry, I was mad at how much life had changed, about all the things I couldn't do and all the extra responsibilities I had to take on at work. I was just mad at the world and the shitty state it was in, but anger ultimately only hurts yourself and you must let it go.

The next stage is bargaining and to be honest I never found this one applied with grief, I knew that grieving is a process and there are no shortcuts, it just takes time, generally a year or more for someone you really loved. For the pandemic I accepted early on that I had no real control over how long it lasts, I knew it would be a year or more. The only thing I'll say is how barging works in a pandemic (for example I'll be safe if I stay around people who are healthy). That is one of the scary parts of COVID-19; a person could be around you, have no symptoms and still be a carrier and pass it on. I'll admit that while I was careful with work and did not get within six feet of friends in months (in truth two friends I have not seen in person now in over six months), for my Mom I did make an exception. I explained to her that since she was in a different household that I shouldn't see her, but her reply was that she would rather die than not see her children (this is especially true now since my dad passed on three years ago). So, I did go and see her. While it may have been some bargaining, it was her choice and I was certain she had not left the house in months, and her chances of having it were close to zero.

Despair is the fourth and this one I certainly felt. When I first entered self-isolation (with my wife—I was never alone thankfully) it was strange but bearable as I have always enjoyed time to myself. I started writing this book, reading, exercising, and generally doing things I enjoy. What brought on some negative feelings for me came at two points. The first was on March 25th when we did have to close our business (although we were open again for curb-side pickup, and mail and courier orders on April 2nd). At that point I was concerned about how long we would be closed, how I would pay bills (I am not eligible for unemployment due to being an owner) and ultimately what would happen to our business. Now I can say my fears were irrational and we are fine, but it didn't feel like it back then. The other time I felt despair was late May to early June. I was just mentally exhausted from doing a lot of work/jobs I wasn't used to doing and being so busy with only a few of us at work (usually we have twelve staff but for over 2 months we had only six). I was missing simple stuff like movies, get-togethers, going to restaurants, and other regular activities that I had not done in months. I love to travel and the thought of not being able to go anywhere (for a while even outside of my own town) for a year or more was disheartening. Even now I must accept that I won't be going anywhere warm in the winter of 2021. Another thing I love is going to conventions (as an author I have often had a table at them as well to sell my books) and when one convention after another got cancelled, I was disappointed. For a while it felt like there was almost nothing to look forward to; no new movies, no concerts, no festivals, no parties, all the regular social activities that I enjoyed were either canceled or put on a long or extended hold.

The fifth stage is acceptance and that is something I certainly came to feel by the summertime here in Newfoundland (when we had almost no cases) and now in December when we are back in the twenties. COVID-19 is scary, no disputing that and I always feel a little twinge in my stomach whenever I hear of more cases in my province. There are times when I am in a store or supermarket and I wonder, does the person next to me have it? Did they just pick up the same apple I did? Ultimately you must quiet those thoughts, or they will consume you and your worrying will never stop.

While four vaccines have currently been approved in Canada (and the United Kingdom), I have accepted that COVID-19 will be around for some time to come (Health Canada, 2021.) Christmas 2020 was different for me. I did not see friends like I did other years. Simple things like the gift exchange we have with friends every year just did not happen. I am fortunate in a way that I do have a small family and to be honest, the people I want to see on a regular basis I do already. The idea of "coming home" for Christmas does not apply to me, I am already home and there are cousins who I will most likely never see again (even first ones who live in US) and I am fine with that. COVID-19 is such a strange and stubborn thing, you get some great news (like Pfzier-BioNTech being approved for people ages twelve and up in Canada) but Nova Scotia and all of Ontario were sent back into lockdown in May of 2021. We got out of our second lockdown in March but then in May part of the province went back to Level 4. By the end of May everyone ages twelve and up can register to get their first vaccine shot, over fifty percent of the population here has had that same shot, yet the threat of more lockdowns still looms, and we are told to avoid parties and large get-togethers. One of the vaccines (which millions of people around the world want) has a small chance of causing blood clots, so there are other people who refuse to take it and government (when possible) instead gives people one of the other three. It is such a huge task vaccinating the whole world (and keeping outbreaks at bay) that is always going to be two steps forward, one step back kind of deal in terms of ending the pandemic. From what I know even after I receive both shots there is a strong likelihood that I will have to get a booster shot next year and that COVID-19 will continue to have an impact on all lives to some extent in 2022.

I think with COVID while we must be careful (wear masks, wash hands more often, get flu shots, social distance, and everything else the government instructs us to do), life must also go on. As more people are cured, eventually life will return to normal sometime in 2021, I believe. I also firmly believe that COVID-19 will ultimately make us a better world and society. We have shown (at least the sensible people) that we can come together and help each other out in a crisis. The government (at least here in Canada) does have our best interest at heart, and we can trust them to control/reduce the spread of the virus and protect us. I hope after this we will all be more aware of how hard medical professionals work to keep us safe and look after us when we are sick. If nothing else with these practices ingrained in us of better hygiene, distancing, and less handshaking we will all get colds and flus less often. In an economic sense I think it will show for many of us how fragile our economy is and how much we take the services around us for granted. As someone who had their business shut down, I certainly see how the world can change drastically overnight and you really do need to hope for the best but prepare for the worst. I know for me personally I have a greater appreciation for what is produced locally, I am going to always try to buy and support local wherever I can. We will get through this; I think we are already through the worst of it. I think in the post-COVID world we will be kinder to each other, more considerate, and come to realize that everything about this world is fragile. Appreciate what you have, what you can do and the people around you. Find pleasure in the simple things and try to not to take anything for granted. And if you can find some stylish masks (I personally have two with Superman and two with Marvel comic book characters on them), why not wear them and show other people not only that you care about their safety but that you will always have your own style and interests.

Chapter 6: Travel

I have been fortunate in my life with lots of things and for this chapter I'll focus on how I've been traveling my entire life (even when I couldn't remember it). This year, 2020, (and most likely 2021) will be a little different with COVID-19 but as I am drawing on past experiences (and discussing where I would like to go in the future) it should not be a big change. My parents started taking me to Florida, USA when I was just six months old. I do not have any memories of Florida until age six or seven, and even then, they are vague. I used to have an undying love for Florida but in recent years I have become more woke (as they say) and I can certainly see what Florida is really like, especially since Trump became president. You might have heard it before; travel is the best education, and I am making the case that it is indeed true. This chapter will primarily be about the fun, unusual, serious, eye-opening, surprising, and most positive experiences I have had with the many places I have been. Also, as usual I will reference some articles and try to come up with recommendations and advice for my lovely readers to follow. If you hate travel and are content to never leave your hometown (and I do know people like this), then this chapter might not be for you.

I have got to start with some serious (and disturbing) experiences I've had while traveling. They opened my eyes to the way the world really is. My parents used to have a house in Florida (in fact for about a year we had two, as it took a long time to sell one) and we would go there at least once a year, sometimes twice. This happened quite some time ago (about thirty years) and I'll admit I didn't act the way I should have, but in my defense, I was only fourteen and was unprepared for the situation. I live in Newfoundland. It is a small place that is still predominantly white (though I am glad to see more immigrants and people of color have been showing up over the past ten or so years). When we bought this house in a trailer park where everyone else was white, I did not think anything of it. Our house sat on the top of a small hill. I remember we had a small back yard, a view of the channel, steps that lead down to a boat house, and even a tiny beach. If I left the house, I could walk to a regular full-sized beach in about fifteen minutes. It was a safe area, and I would often walk by myself.

One year we were down for our winter getaway (my brother and I would just miss two weeks of school, and in my opinion, it never hurt either of us) and I noticed a Black couple had moved in a few doors down. It was unusual as they were the only ones, but they kept to themselves and the most interaction I had with them was a smile and a wave, which was good with me. After about four days I noticed I didn't see this Black couple anymore. It seemed odd, from what I knew these mobile homes were either bought or rented a month at a time. Another day or so later, the mobile park manager showed up at our place. We knew her, but this was nonetheless unusual for her to just come over for no reason. As a teen, I was not prepared for what the park manager said next. She calmly explained that we may have noticed a Black couple had been around this week. We all nodded and said yes, and she continued. She told us not to worry that they're gone, and we don't put up with their kind around here (her words). I was shocked, it was one of those moments where I just froze, I did not know what to do say or do. My parents got curious and asked how she could do that without breaking any laws. She replied that as the park manager she simply made up a rule and then pretended they broke it, so if anyone checked it would be legal. After that there was just idle chit-chat and she left shortly afterwards. Even writing this now some thirty years later it still bothers me. She was blatantly racist and was in a position of power to throw people out of the park. I thought later that if this happened then, it must have been happening for years. As far as I know this woman never faced any consequences for her actions and that's plain wrong, criminal even. It gave me the knowledge that racism is sadly alive and well in the US (not just the south as recent events have shown) and Black people are often at a disadvantage in many parts of the world. To be clear, I am not saying there aren't racists everywhere, many years later I heard it here in Newfoundland, this was just something that travel exposed me to at a young age, one of the ugly truths of the world.

About twenty-five years ago (when I was nineteen) I had a much more positive experience while traveling and I'm happy to relate that here. Here in Newfoundland, we are known for being friendly. I've seen and experienced this first-hand. But for now, I'll talk about Mexico and how warm and friendly the Mexican people I've met are. My dad had a friend in Texas and one year we decided to drive to Texas and then go to Mexico. This friend, (I will call him Ryan), used to visit Mexico all the time and had become good friends with a family in a small town. Ryan did a lot for this family and even helped the daughter go to school in Texas on a student exchange program (she would eventually marry his son). We went to this small town named Montecado. We went to this family's house, were sold some cheap Corona beer and then myself and my brother were handed over to the two older sisters who showed us around their hometown. They took us to a bar, introduced us to their brother and showed us where the school gym was in case, we wanted to play basketball. They were honestly some of the friendliest and warmest people I had ever met. At the time I had never had a girlfriend and had little contact with women in any kind of non-family situation. So, receiving all this attention from a young, attractive Mexican woman was flattering to me and it made me feel good. I got to see how most Mexicans were hard-working, friendly people that welcomed strangers with open arms. It made me see just how much I had and how little many people in this Mexican town did. The whole experience left a positive impression in my mind.

I read an article about why travel is the best education and I have to say it has a lot of accurate and even insightful things to say. It's appropriately called "10 Reasons Why Traveling Is The Best Form of Education" and I hope you'll check it out. The article's first point is languages. When you travel to somewhere where the primarily language is not English, you quickly pick up a few words and phrases. You learn what you need to learn like asking, where is the bathroom? I was fortunate to visit Paris, France when I was in high school. I only took French for the bare minimum time in school (for me that meant until I was fourteen), and I just never had the interest (or the knack) for learning another language. I discovered in just a few days in Paris I was speaking French phrases for the first time in my life. I remember back then thinking that the only way I would ever learn a second language would be by living in a place where that language was spoken exclusively.

The article also of course talks about the importance of immersing yourself in other cultures (which you do when you stay anywhere for more than a few days), and I certainly agree with that. Traveling gives you the chance to connect with nature in different ways (outside of large cities of course) and gain an appreciation for all the beauty the environment can offer and delight you with. I went to Alaska with my wife and parents about five years ago on a cruise out of Vancouver (which I would highly recommend if you like cruises) and got to see some beautiful places and animals. I got to watch a black bear calmly play in a river just below us (it was a tour, and we were on a wooden bridge above the river). This was in a protected park and black bears could not be hunted, so it didn't have the usual fear of people. What made it special and unique was that it was acting as any bear would. When we first arrived and walked to one of several lookout spots on the bridge there was no bear. The guide advised us to wait and after about five minutes a black bear wandered down from somewhere behind us in the woods. He glanced at this group of people a few times but overall, just accepted our presence. The guide explained that the bears were fattening up for winter (this was in September), and we watched as he purposefully got a fish out of the river, ripped the head off and went on to another. The guide further explained that the brains of the salmon were the fattest, tastiest part of the fish and therefore had the most calories. While it looked wasteful at first, we quickly saw that birds (seagull, crows and others I didn't know) would follow the bear and eat all the dead fish. We just stood there for a good half hour or more and watched animals in their natural habit. It was a simple, beautiful moment that I will always remember. It made you see the extent to which wild animals need their habitats and how, in my opinion, they should never be hunted.

During that same Alaskan trip, we went to see a glacier (we got to see several, which was nice) and on the bus ride there our driver talked about the environment. He was probably in his fifties, and he talked about how much the weather had changed in Alaska since he was a boy. There were warmer temperatures, more rain, less snow, the changing patterns of fish during mating season. He chalked it up to climate change (correctly) and warned us of how we need to do better. Sadly, no one spoke up and he signed off, but his point stuck with me. Soon after that I got a Prius hybrid and I thought about how much the weather has changed where I live. While we can still get a lot of snow, overall we see more rain, wind, and extreme weather than we ever did before. That is the great part about travel; it opens your eyes up to what is going on in world outside of your town, it makes you see that we all live on this planet, and we are all affected by things like climate change.

Some of the other important points brought up by this article is that traveling forces you to be more social, to interact with strangers, and to do new things. Something I really loved that I first did on vacation in Florida was zip lining. The place we went to really made you do everything on your own. You were given a safety demonstration, signed a form, were given your harness, a metal clip, and a cord, and did every step yourself. Once you conquered your fear (like some people I have a fear of heights) it was really an adrenaline rush, and the view was great. I was tired by the end of our zip lining, but I was so glad I did it.

I used to be a shy person (I still am a little at times) but when I traveled, I was forced to ask people directions. I asked how a subway system works in terms of which way I was headed (London has the best one I've been on), and I came out of my shell. That same trip in London I planned a day to do things I wanted while my wife went off with another couple who were traveling with us. Spending time by yourself in a different city (and in this case another country) is a great experience and I loved every minute of it (I even won four hundred pounds playing poker), something I could not imagine myself doing some twenty years before as a shy seventeen-year-old.

In my experience the world is full of regular people who are friendly and will help you if you ask politely. We were once in Nashville, Tennessee on a family trip while we were driving all the way back from Vancouver. This was long before the days of Google maps or even GPS, so when we stopped for gas, my dad asked some guys in the truck next to us for directions. We had tickets to the Grand Ole Opry (a bluegrass/country music show, not something I would normally see) and they offered to show us most of the way there. Most people would have just explained, or maybe even have drawn a map, but they drove for a good ten to fifteen minutes until we could see a sign that said "Grand Ole Opry" before they turned off. It was nice of them and a good example of southern hospitality. When I think about it now, we really were trusting them. Back then we didn't have cell phones (this was 1989) and really, they could have led us anywhere and things could have turned out poorly, but they didn't. We got to the Grand Ole Opry fine and had a nice time and I learned that sometimes you really can depend on the kindness of strangers.

This brings me to the last two points of the article; learning about yourself and compassion for others. When you travel you get to see all kinds of people, and as in virtually every city (but perhaps more so in larger ones) you get to see the depths of despair some homeless people fall into and how even children are often there with them. One of my wife's cousins decided to have her wedding (and honeymoon) at a resort in Cuba. I thought it was a great idea and like I am with any trip, I was excited to go, especially somewhere I had never been to before. Cuba was an interesting place; Havana was a mixture of old and new buildings and that's where this story takes place. We were staying at a resort and decided to take a guided tour into the city, stopping along the way to see an old Spanish fort and a cafe on the side of the road with a truly incredible view of the wooded valley below. We had a nice tour of the city, I got to visit a room Ernest Hemingway once lived in (I have also been to his house in Key West, Florida many times), had a good lunch and eventually ended up searching for a particular kind of cigar one of the people in our tour wanted to bring home. Before I get to that, however, I must add what happened with a couple of young boys who were begging for money on a street corner. The homeless can be a little tricky. I have always read (and seen interviews) that the worst thing you can do is give them money, this is because most of them are on the street due to addiction problems and money just helps them get their next fix. That said you're not often walking around with food, clothing or other essential items on you, so money is just the only thing you can give on most occasions.

In Cuba there were two younger boys (maybe eleven or twelve years old) with their hands open, asking for money. One of the men in the group was generous, opened his wallet and gave one of them a twenty-dollar bill (US money). I am sure his thought was that they would buy something together and enjoy it. Instead, what happened was the boys started yelling, pushing, shoving and eventually punching each other. We were all shocked but with no police or any other authority figure nearby, there was nothing we could do besides keep walking. Our guide soon explained to that of course the US dollar is worth a lot more than the Cuban dollar and that could have been the most money either of them had seen in years, if ever. So, in a sad twist of fate what should have been a kind gesture ending up just making the man feel worse and made me realize that sometimes no matter what your intentions are, it's just not possible to help everyone you see on the street. Once I went to a convention and nearby there was a homeless woman (this was in Columbus, Ohio). Rather than money I gave her several granola bars (yes, I'm that kind of person who does prepare and brings snacks with them, especially by myself on holiday). I hope that she ate them, but it was an unusual experience as she clearly looked surprised and never even said thank you.

To return to the Cuba story, we were looking for this special cigar for one guest and it got harder and harder as the day wore on. We went in stores, went up to street vendors, even stopped in alleyways and people's houses as our guide tried incessantly to get this kind of cigar. This is something I am a little embarrassed to admit but I think the experience and the analysis is worth it. As we got deeper into the city and away from all the tourists (besides our small group) I felt more and more uncomfortable. The streets had more garbage, the amount of homeless people increased, and I saw two men both unconscious on the sidewalks with wet streaks on their pants making it obvious they drank enough to piss themselves (I've never done this, and I don't ever plan to). Suffice it to say I became more and more nervous, got closer to my wife, and could feel the hairs rise on the back of my neck and the tension in my mind grow. We did eventually find the right cigar and got back to the van (and the resort) without incident. At the time I was mad at the guide for taking us to these back streets and quite angry at the person who wanted this specific cigar for putting us on the journey in this first place. Thinking back on it now, I was just wrong. My wife assured me that we were in no danger (she was right) and that I should just think of it as an adventure (which was also true). More importantly though some people live below the poverty lines. My feelings of apprehension were brought about by my own bias and sheltered life that hid me from an experience such as this.

Most of us have a fear of change (and I do), as you grow up and age many things change, including yourself. When you travel to somewhere different and are put in situations you've never dealt with before you are faced with a change of circumstance, a snippet of the world that is different from how you understand it, and it scares you because it makes you acknowledge that we live in a big world and one part of the world can be different than another. If I really look around, I can see more poverty here in Newfoundland than I did before. Hopefully, travel has opened my eyes to notice the world better with all its cracks and imperfections. As I write this, much of the world is still in the throes of a pandemic and travel has been greatly reduced, if not stopped completely for millions of people. I love to travel, and I know I will miss it in the months (hopefully not years) to come. I will miss all the options I am usually presented with for travel but in some ways it's a blessing as it will get me to explore my own province and country more than I have before.

The last part of the article talks about how travel forces you to learn about yourself and I would be remiss if I did not comment on it. Travel for me has helped me to learn better what I really want. For a long time, trips to me often meant a chance to get stuff like comics, miniatures, books and of course get away from the cold winter weather. I've come to see travel in a much different way lately. It lets you see what it is you truly enjoy. While you want to do many of same things you do at home while on vacation (get groceries, go to movies, ordinary stuff) you also get the thrill of doing new activities (and ones I can't do at home like have alcohol in a movie theater). The choices of what activities you do on vacation reveal the things you truly love and perhaps even indicate changes you should make in your life (which for me will include moving away from Newfoundland so I can do different activities). I crave a routine in my life wherever I go. I love to ride my bike and I find now that I am planning where we stay based partly on how close is to a bike trail (and of course that the area has a bike rental shop). I want to find vegetarian restaurants with good ratings in the area (as I have been a vegetarian for over fourteen years as I write this) and in the past few years I found a place that sells CBD products (which I quite enjoy). I actively look for casinos whenever I travel, I'll always make a point to go to local comic book stores (I have been reading them for over thirty years now).

I'm such an enthusiast of Dungeons and Dragons (D&D) that I've done lots of role-playing sessions with strangers both at conventions and in comic book stores. I have got to meet a few of my geeky heroes (including Stan Lee, George R. R. Martin, and Steve Jackson) because I made certain to be in cities at the right dates in order to go to conventions (or at least made sure I had tickets when we would be in the place anyway). I can even say that while on vacation in the Bahamas there were just two other people on a beach (besides my wife and I) and one of them was from Newfoundland (the wife recognized my accent and asked me where I was from).

I think most importantly to me personally I have learned that travel is something I have come to enjoy more than gifts or money. You get a gift and while you love it and may use it for years, it will eventually just become junk or some old dusty things that is never touched, used, or even seen. When you travel you collect memories and experiences and that is something that will last your whole life. Travel as much as you can, go wherever it's safe (without going bankrupt of course) and see the world for how it really is. Sadly, I must add that if you're reading this in

2021, it may still not be a good time to go anywhere outside your town. COVID-19 has changed the world and its impact will go on for years if not decades to come. People are exploring more of their own neighborhoods on bikes (a local bike shop called Canary Cycles has done better than ever the past year) and nature is responding to less noise and traffic (Fears, 2020). People all over the US are hearing bird singing more than they ever have before. The reason is simple of course, as less cars, trucks and planes are in use in big cities and people are home more to hear the birds and notice them. While I love to travel, I would encourage everyone who reads this to find something you love about your hometown and do it more often, most especially if that involves a park or trail to wander on.

One of the most important things travel will show you (if you go outside of say the US and Canada for example) is the huge divide between a first world and third world country. We take so much for granted here in Canada, when you go to a place like Jamaica you see how other people live. While we were there as part of a stop on a cruise, they showed us a spot where people lived in caves. It was one those surreal moments that are hard to accept but it is the kind of thing I needed to see to open my eyes to how great the wealth divide has become. I know there are homeless people everywhere but seeing people living in caves was shocking. I think another important thing I have discovered from traveling is that money is not what makes you happy. I have met people from countries like Mexico who are happy, friendly and generous, even though they have few possessions or money. We would perhaps call many people in third world countries poor but is that really the case? Maybe once wealth and possessions are not in the equation, we can discover what happiness really means, it is something I often wonder about. I am a firm believer that traveling will broaden your mind in ways formal education cannot. It will make you a better person and it will show you not only how other people find happiness but hopefully the best way you can do so for yourself.

Chapter 7: University

I went to university for a long time, about nine years in total. I know people who have doctorates, many different degrees, or medical doctors who went longer but I think most people would agree that is a significant amount of time. For people with no patience, I will say that while university was not a waste of time (at least for me) it did not help me get the career I wanted. Do I blame all that on Memorial University of Newfoundland (MUN)? No, not completely of course, but I think they can take some blame.

One article I found on the topic states that university cannot guarantee you will get a good job or have a wonderful career (Stevenson, 2020). What university does do for almost everyone is important though; it helps their social life/social skills by leaps and bounds. University is a place where you expand your horizons and increase your knowledge, but just as importantly you grow as a person, you find your tribe. I was something of an outcast in school (I think of myself more of a geek than a nerd, but I think I was called both) and while I had friends, I do agree that until university I never felt that I fit in well with any class or even any group (besides my group of personal friends). Once I got to MUN I was still a shy, withdrawn person. University did not change me overnight, it took years. I would say that it was really towards the end of my degree (I was twenty-three then) that I had become a more outgoing/likable/friendly person. But I'm skipping ahead.

What I loved about university life right away was that the little groups (or cliques as I have heard them called when I was in high school), were gone. I did occasionally have class with someone from my high school (or even a friend) but for the most part I was in classes with strangers—a lot of strangers—and it was both an exciting and yet still intimidating prospect. I am not sure what it's like anymore but when I was at MUN in 1994, it was at least a little bit of a party school. A bunch of my friends were in the math society (including me and a few others who weren't even doing Math) and they had a lot of mixers and pub crawls, and it was generally a nice place to hang out. There was usually a good chance of finding someone there I knew. It is worth pointing out here how unusual MUN was. Think about it, the Math society had more mixers and pub crawls than almost every other society! I used to spend many a Friday night at MUN going around to several mixers, getting cheap drinks (sometimes too many) and ending up either downtown with friends or going to a movie.

In high school I was a loner for most of the time. I barely joined any clubs or groups and if I did, I did not stick with them. I think for me I had such negative feelings associated with my high school that doing anything to spend more time there made no sense. When I got to MUN I soon discovered there were groups I would enjoy and people I had a lot in common with. I joined the Star Trek Society, yes at MUN they were a real group that got ratified and received funding from the student council every year. I joined a Tae Kwan Do group (though in truth I had been doing it before, I just went to it at MUN as it was more convenient) and I went to the university gym. Later when I lost interest in Tae Kwon Do I joined another group at MUN called Diversified Combat Systems (you guessed it, martial arts). All these groups lead to friendships, good times, job opportunities, movies, brief TV appearances and most importantly a chance to edit a club newsletter. Eventually I did virtually the whole thing, including most of the content. I joined a Monty Python comedy club; they didn't have a lot of meetings but were always sending out group e-mails and had lots of friendly people in it. *Bitters* (a university bar that did cool stuff like movie and trivia nights) was a bar where older, more mature graduate students would go but was a place I started going to when I was twenty.

I joined a group that was somewhat outside my comfort zone, a student newspaper. I would never call myself a reporter (I did not have the interest in it) but I went to meetings, had lunch in their break room, and got to know some new people. I'll admit I wanted some public attention and I wanted to get free stuff; *The Muse* (the name of MUN's student paper) provided all that. I was an entertainment writer and I got free CDs (this was the '90s remember, with no way to legally buy digital music) and got to watch movies for free. I could go to a movie whenever I wanted and even bring a friend, if I did a review afterwards. I will be honest 90% of the reviews I did were terrible; little of what I wrote got published. I even went so far to go on trip to Nova Scotia to a kind of student newspaper conference. It was here I realized journalism was not for me and neither was *The Muse*. You see, at 19, I was still shy and really had a hard time mixing with people in social situations (I'm still not much better. I generally wait for someone to talk to me at any kind of party with strangers). This conference involved getting up early one day to participate in a panel discussion with other student papers from different universities. I was invited to a party in someone's dorm room (I was lucky that I knew someone staying at Saint Francis Xavier University, otherwise who knows where I would have slept!) and was told everyone from *The Muse* would be there.

I didn't go to the party as I figured it would just be awkward. I didn't drink yet, and it would make getting to the meeting that much harder since it started at 9:00 a.m. So that meeting for the first half hour I was the only one there to represent *The Muse*. Keep in mind that I had only been in the group a few months. I did not know the answer to a single question and just replied "no comment" to all of them. Finally, two people showed up, out of breath, disheveled and obviously hungover from the night before. They answered the remaining questions and the dreadful meeting ended. I can see now looking back that I should have gone to the party and forgotten about the meeting, it would have forced me out of my shell a little sooner. In those days, however, I was focused, withdrawn, and probably not a lot of fun to be around at times. While I stuck with *The Muse* for a while after that, it was the beginning of the end as I just did not fit in socially with most of them.

Once I was finished my first two years or so at MUN (it took me a while to make up my mind on a degree path) I got to take courses I was really interested in, ones I enjoyed a lot. I ended up doing English and Philosophy first and later Education. One elective course that stands out is a Folklore class I did that focused on tattoos, body building, and piercings. While at the time I had no piercings or tattoos (I got two tattoos eventually) the fact that this could be a course was fascinating to me. Of course, one day the discussion led to the professor asking if anyone in the class had tattoos. It turned out people did the course (at least seven or eight of them) in part because they loved tattoos and piercings. One attractive woman with short green hair got up and started to pull her shirt off with her back to the class (the professor came quickly over to help cover her). I was really surprised someone would be so forward with essentially a bunch of strangers. She had the most amazing tattoo that started at the base of her neck and went all the way to the base of her spine. It was a green dragon, and the detail was incredible. I talked to her a couple of times after class, but thinking about it now, I cringe thinking how awkward I was. I never said anything offensive, I just did not know what to say to women, even at twenty they were still quite a mystery to me. I remember she had a homemade cloth kind of purse and never wore shoes (or socks); I wish I had made more of an effort to get to know her. But at twenty I had a big problem in that while I would be attracted to a woman and might want to date her, I was so afraid of rejection that I would never ask one out.

I could see that I had some views that might not be considered the most forward thinking, perhaps I was even a little sexist. There was this course in women's studies that was cross listed with Philosophy (which meant it counted as both) and I decided to take it. The course was good for me as it not only put me in contact with a lot of women (it was filled with about 90% women) but it also helped me see all the injustices and sexist attitudes women had to deal with every day. This would have been in maybe 1996 and I learned about the wage gap still present for women (including in Canada and locally in Newfoundland) and how many women put up with terrible behavior from men in their lives. I also got to be in a group with some other students (all women) and I enjoyed getting to know them. I had few female friends, and it did me a lot of good.

I also watched a video of a woman giving birth in this Women's Studies class. I know this was supposed to give me an appreciation for the miracle of life but all it did was make me feel a great deal more respect for mothers. Well, that and it also helped to cement in my mind the fact that I never wanted kids. For that class I was in a group for an assignment with three women. It wasn't a big deal; I am always friendly, and we all got along but they certainly helped me see I had male privilege and how I needed to learn to see the world from a woman's point of view.

MUN wasn't just a big lesson for me on women and relationships though, as I hinted at earlier, I had a lot of trouble making up my mind on what do to academically and doing a variety of courses certainly helped me choose. I quickly discovered that I hated anything to do with numbers, business, languages, or politics. MUN gave me a chance to rediscover my love of literature and writing. I was getting prepared for an English exam, and I realized this was not a chore at all, it was enjoyable to skim through books I loved. While I was not a great student, I was good, sometimes excellent, but not consistently so. I took my course work seriously, was almost never late with an assignment and always had the readings done (well, at least after my first three semesters). It was a pleasure once I got past the required English courses to do ones that interested me. I was lucky that there were courses in both Sci-Fi/fantasy and horror fiction while I was there. I loved both and had the pleasure of having a professor who was considered a world expert on Dracula (the historical figure, not the fictional fanged man). I can honestly say I would never have written this book (or my Newfoundland Vampire series) if it were not for my degree in English. I received a letter from the English department for getting an "A" in a course and was told by a professor I should pursue a masters in English.

Another important experience I had at university was failure and facing disappointment. For my school career up until the end of high school I had little to no difficulty with courses. I never knew what it meant to fail a subject or repeat something but that was about to change. At MUN I failed courses (not a lot but enough for it to sting) and I realized that while I was good at memorizing facts, I didn't do a good job with understanding concepts and ultimately, I found that even my ability to memorize was severely affected by my interest level in a subject. I got better as a student and took my lumps by dropping out of courses I was told I would fail, doing two courses twice, and getting a tutor to help me with grammar, German, and stats (back then you could do an arts degree and avoid math completely by doing courses in a second language). I will admit, however, that I was easily distracted (and still am) and was never good at following rules for citing quotes or doing up a list of references at the end.

After doing two courses in Shakespeare, I was told by a professor that I should do a Masters in English as I displayed a lot of interest (he was a great professor and quite a character). So, I went to the head of English Graduate Studies and showed him my marks. He was pleasant but told me the truth, my marks just weren't there and there was no point applying to do a master's degree in English. I remember he used the words "You have fits of inspiration," which was true. There were times when I felt productive and came up with great ideas. Sadly, most of those times didn't get me an A in many courses and no matter how hard I tried I only did get one A in any English course. It hurt to accept that I would never be a university professor (as I did think for years would happen), but it was an important life lesson. It stung but I am glad he told me the truth as applying and then being rejected would have hurt even more. Everyone is faced with failure, it is not failing that's the bad part, it's how you move forward and learn from your mistakes. I came up with a compromise. I wanted to teach so if I could not teach at university, I could teach at trade schools and that led me to do a diploma and a master's degree in education.

I have also always loved a good argument or discussion. I still call my friend John once a week to chat (and he's someone I met at university). Here in Newfoundland, I guess you could call me a gab bag. One of the last courses I did for my bachelor's degree was a philosophy course on Plato which dealt primarily with love, moral behavior, and the pursuit of happiness. At that time, I had started dating my girlfriend (now my wife) and I was falling in love. Suffice it to say I was curious about what the professor (and the book) had to say. To sum it up basically he would say that you need someone to complete you, someone who would aid you in a journey to become the best version of yourself, and I have got to say it fit. That course was also a great example of what happens when you don't pay attention. The professor said the exam was open book, but I still saw other students cramming as much as they could before the exam. I paid attention and worked all semester, so I was drunk and at a party the night before (and still got an A in the course).

Doing a diploma and a master's in education were great experiences. By that point I had finally become good at being a student. I was more outspoken in class, well-organized, and I got more "A"s then I did before. Earlier I talked about nine years at Memorial, but this was not all the same time. When I finished my diploma in Adult Education (along with my bachelor's degree), I went out into the working world and found that the only job I could get related to teaching was being a student assistant and doing some tutoring at an after-school help center. To explain, a student assistant does little to no teaching. Basically, you are with a child in the k-12 system who needs help to get through the day. That could mean any number of things from developmental, to physical challenges, to learning disabilities, to behaviors linked to other personality disorders. It was only after doing this for three years (and discovering it was not for me) that I went back to Memorial to do my masters.

While education does give you the opportunity to learn how to teach and engage students, it also gives you a lot of chances for self-analysis and self-reflection. One course had an assignment where you looked at major events in your life and did a timeline of your accomplishments. At that point I was married and almost finished my master's, and my life looked pretty good on paper. I also did an assignment that got you to think about what your life would have been like if you made different choices; if I never went to university at all for example, and instead got a job right away. It made me realize how much I had grown as a person and how I would have been in many ways a lot lesser of a person if I had not been there.

I also must mention a particular course in education where I really got to know my other students and had a friendly, fun, and creative professor. We talked about our feelings in class and even devoted one class to how we all deal with the loss of a loved one. Both my parents were alive then, but I had lost my aunt Andy in 1999, and it bothered me for years afterwards. She was an example of someone gone too soon (she died in her 50's) and what made it even worse was that it was preventable. She had had cancer years before and having undergone treatment and surgery, just never went back for a checkup for eight years. By the time she did finally go back she was full of cancer, and it was too late. While I did not tear up in class, other people did, and it was a nice bonding experience. We did things like play a song that had a lot of personal meaning for us (mine was *The Sunscreen Song* which I still love and listen to a lot). At the graduate level I was also amazed (and quite pleased) that we spent multiple classes watching and discussing the movie *Shrek*. If you really look at it, you'll see it has deeper meaning and a really wonderful soundtrack. It was the first (and only time) I could say that I was a straight A student, and I did feel proud of the work I did in my courses.

It is time to talk about one of the negative things that happened to me at MUN. I had just one semester left of my master's and had to decide between a large assignment (a thesis as it is called in academic circles) and a practicum (work term), with a shorter paper (40-60 pages). To help me make the decision I decided to visit the head of graduate studies for education at MUN. I don't remember her name, but she was an unpleasant woman. She told me right away that I needed to come up with something unique for a thesis. At this point I had been talking with another professor for months and I felt I already had a unique and interesting idea, but this prof was immediately dismissive of it. She then told me some people felt I never should have been accepted in the master's program! I did not have any teaching experience and that teaching was probably not for me. I was in shock and hurt, I do not even remember what I said, I was so surprised. I just remember feeling embarrassed and got out of there as soon as I could. Think about what this meant, I was one semester (4 months) away from being finished and she said I never should have started in the first place! Aside from being mean it was also a terrible thing to say to a student who had invested years of their life and was about to enter the teaching field! I would have hated being in one of her classes. I guess she was more into the crushing dreams and lowering self-esteem business than any positive teaching notion.

But that's enough negativity. I don't know if I was ever meant to be an instructor, but I did have some great experiences. I taught communications and ran an English writing center at the College of the North Atlantic (CNA) in Grand Falls-Windsor (central Newfoundland) for a year, did some short-term teaching at Compu College, and Academy Canada (both in St. John's). I remember first going out to Grand Falls-Windsor (GFW) in September, and I was excited. It was my first teaching job and my first time living off the Avalon Peninsula (where most people live in Newfoundland. It has two cities and some big towns). Even though GFW is a small town it was fun to explore, meet new people, and establish a new routine.

Ultimately while I think was a good instructor, I made some wrong choices and it finished my teaching career, really before it ever even started. Newfoundland is a strange place in that most people who teach (outside of the university level) usually must put in time outside the St. John's area before they can come back to where they want to teach. People want to teach where they are from (usually) and that often means getting seniority, so you can attain that position. I am from the St. John's area (Conception Bay South), so that is where I wanted to end up naturally. I thought a year in GFW was enough, but I was wrong. I also didn't realize that once you turn down a position with College of the North Atlantic, there's no getting back in. I was offered to return to Academy Canada once but by then I had already moved on and accepted my fate at our family business.

If I am being honest, I'll say that I am opinionated and always want to do things my way, and that doesn't always go over well with students and authority figures. I suppose I always wanted to be the boss, the one to make the decisions, but I never wanted all the responsibilities and headaches that come with it, and you cannot have it both ways.

To conclude (and I have to, there's lots more I could say about MUN but this is enough), I'll say that I am glad I went to MUN as it gave me wonderful experiences, helped me grow as a person, expanded my knowledge and renewed my love of reading and writing. I will add, however, that I do feel that in terms of a career it was a waste of time and money. I cannot put all the blame on MUN, I wanted to do arts and I wanted to do education but there is at least some blame for them, why was I accepted in the master's program in Education with no teaching experience? I can think of an obvious answer, money. Of course, I am speculating, and I will never know, in truth I do not remember the requirements, it could have easily been the case that while teaching experience was preferred it was not essential Perhaps that horrible professor was right; if I had never been accepted into the master's program in education, I would have been forced to make a different choice. My life would have been different. But would it have been better? That I will never know.

What I do know and can say is that anyone now who asked me if they should go to MUN I would say they should think long and hard about it. For me it was just assumed that I would go; I did well in school, I enjoyed some classes so why not continue? That should not be an automatic decision for anyone. I would say if you are prepared to truly embrace academic life and work really hard, get a doctorate, and teach there, then sure. Or if you want to do something practical like teaching, (to be clear, not the way I did it. I can see now getting experience teaching before doing a master's may be the better way). Engineering, nursing, or medicine are also great choices. If you are not sure though, then why not take time and travel, work, think about what you really want? It might seem like it will put you behind but that's a lie, people now often have two or three careers and MUN doesn't have to be a part of your journey either. If, however, you are lucky enough to have the time and money to go to university and just grow as a person and learn for a few years without worrying about a career, then go. MUN made me a better person, it just did not put me on a career path that worked for me. MUN filled me with (mostly) positive memories, and I certainly do not regret my time there. Like most people, I'm just left to wonder about the road not taken and where it might have led me.

Chapter 8: The Internet

The Internet was not something I grew up with. I barely knew it existed until 1994, when I started at MUN. Many people reading this are accustomed to looking something up on the net, whether it is a movie, what time the mall opens, where the new doctor's office is or even just the weather. Before all that I had to check the newspaper, look in a phone book, or call around. I remember walking around downtown St. John's taking pictures of when comic book stores were open (not with a smart phone, just a digital camera that took floppy disks!) just so I'd have the information. When I first started at MUN I will admit to becoming fascinated/obsessed with the Internet. For the first two to three years, I only used the Internet for chatting and other non-academic interests. I do have to relate one experience; around '95 I was an active poster on a Star Trek message board (remember this was not web-based, this was a text-based program you use on old computers). I made a post about my favorite author (then Peter David) and asked a question and while I never expected a reply, I got one! I know it is not that incredible (he is not a famous author) but at the time I was really surprised and impressed that you could hear from a celebrity that way.

As the years went by at MUN things changed, I used the Internet for academic reasons. You could look up whether a book was in stock at the library or renew it. Eventually you could read journals online and even cite websites in papers. This brings me to the heart of this chapter; the incredible difference between well researched, valid ideas and facts versus complete nonsense that people believe and pretend is valid/true. So, while I can't claim to be an expert, as a former academic I do have a good idea if a website is presenting a reasonable idea that either could be/is true or just what a wingnut (or at least a uniformed person) says is true and wants you to believe. I also know it is not always as simple as that, and the worst part is that if a celebrity or government official (like Trump) says something on a social media platform, millions of people not only believe it but are prepared to act on it, often to terrible ends.

Here is an example of something horribly untrue that Trump said that can have deadly consequences; he has used the xenophobic term "Kung Flu" many times this summer and it's highly racist and completely untrue as he blames the Corona virus on China (Lee, 2020). This kind of falsehood can lead to even more racism against Chinese (and Asian) people. As the death toll approaches four million from the virus, I do not even like to imagine what the wrong person could do to someone they felt was at fault for it. This is a massive problem. If you can get in someone's head, find a way to manipulate their emotions, then for a lot of people these implanted ideas will overwhelm any intellect or sense of right and wrong. The belief in misinformation often leads to violence and injury, destruction, and just plainly making the world even more messed up than it already is.

What I have come to see is that a major drawback of the Internet is that it is an easier way for people to connect, organize, and spread their ideas than just in person. While gaining members, talking with like-minded people, and spreading ideas sounds great (and harmless) if you're talking about Star Wars, but what happens when your interest is abducting children? Or you want to recruit more people to ISIS or the KKK? You factor in that most people who join a cult or a terrorist group often feel like outcasts, have mental issues, are desperate to make new friends, and feel like they belong somewhere, you see the terrible danger with which the double-edged sword of the Internet has provided our world).

I read an intersecting article on how we have entered a world of ignorance and one of the main causes is our use of the Internet. I will do my best to explain why this article is legitimate rather than false/misleading. When you read it you can easily see the legitimacy by a few simple things: the person who wrote it has relevant credentials (in this case a PhD and is a military officer), has cited credible sources in his article, is not trying to sell anything and does not seem to have any political bias or agenda. The article is called simply "The Age of Ignorance" and I hope you will check it out (there is a link in references). It is telling (and depressing) that this was written originally in 2017, and I would say the world has gotten a lot worse. The US since the pandemic has seen a decline almost comparable to throwing Asian people in detainment camps in the '40s (Editors, 2021).

He makes the excellent point that people now have much shorter attention spans than they did even ten years ago and social media platforms like Twitter cater to that. When you can only use a limited number of characters to write a message (now up to 280) it makes it a lot harder to explain your message, to provide context and present anything other than your opinion. Also mentioned here is the fact that most people still trust what the government says and when a president constantly spouts lies on Twitter, millions of people believe him (Spangler, 2020).

The Internet is a tool, and it can be used for good. On a personal note, it is wonderful that no matter what question pops into my head I can often find an answer in a few minutes or even seconds for something simple. If I am having trouble getting a lawn mower started, I can find a YouTube video to show me what to do, watch it, and fix a problem that may have cost me much more time and money (I'm not, as they say, handy when it comes to doing things around the house but I'm also not totally incompetent). If I want to go to a movie, I can within minutes watch a preview, read a review, see what times it is playing, and decide whether I should go or not. I can order my groceries, any number of other items from Amazon, try to sell a comic on eBay, plan a trip, watch a webcam of a remote beach in Hawaii, or even just something simple like watch someone on Facebook livestream their night at a bar.

The Internet has made the world a less lonely place with video tools like, Zoom, Skype, Google Meet, and FaceTime (all of those are free in one form or another as well) and I will certainly say Zooming with friends made the worst parts of COVID here in Newfoundland a little better. Online learning has been forced to grow, change, and be more widely accepted in 2020. I can also say personally that I have not only met people I only knew through e-mail (once in a large group when I saw Eurythmics in New York City) I also met my wife from a dating site and have now been married for 16 years.

Returning to academics, I used to be an instructor and I was at university a long time, so I have experienced online learning from both perspectives. When online learning first started at MUN it was quite different. I literally used to get one hundred loose leaf sheets for a course that I would have to put together in a binder (these were lecture notes, articles and assignments). When there was a teleconference, you had to call on the phone and get connected by a local operator at MUN. As I was a distance student but still nearby (for education courses only being offered that way) I got to come into the studio (as such) and see how it was done.

On the other hand, when I was an instructor at College of the North Atlantic (CNA) I taught an online course that was an introduction to computers. Yeah, you read that right, if you are doing a course online you would think an introduction to computers would be relatively simple for you. You'd be surprised. I don't remember any names, but I do recall one student having a lot of difficulty with the course. It got to a point where she would call me during office hours to ask me how to complete some tasks. Don't get me wrong, I was happy to answer any questions, it was just surprising to have someone doing a course on computers lack so much knowledge and experience with them.

The ability to download movies, music, images, books, documents, and any other kind of digital media has meant a tremendous reduction in the amount of paper used. Just as a simple example, when I bought a new TV it only came with the most basic instructions; the much larger guide was just on the TV itself that I could read whenever I needed to. While it is certainly true that piracy has had a huge negative impact on both the music and movie industries, in the past few years that has been changing. Personally, I subscribe to Amazon Prime, Netflix, Disney+, and Crave. These streaming services (varying in price but not unreasonable as I got rid of cable TV in our house years ago) provide me with thousands of hours of entertainment. When I see a movie at Cineplex, my local theatre chain, I get a promotion code I can later use for a digital rental of a movie. With a bigger, new TV I'm even more content to stay at home and watch a film. As I have always been a fan of documentaries (and reality shows that provide insight into the world) I have found there is plenty of knowledge to be gained from watching various streaming services. For example, just recently I have been watching *Down to Earth with Zac Efron* on Netflix and while I'm not a huge fan of the actor, the places he goes on the show are quite fascinating and help you see the world from a different perspective.

As I was already paying for Amazon Prime, I also signed up for Amazon Music (it was cheaper for me than Spotify) which means I have access to over six million songs and can easily download them to a device and listen to them anywhere. I enjoy listening to audiobooks more than reading them, and with Audible (I know I am like an ad for Amazon) I always have plenty to listen to. The point being that the urge to illegally download any kind of media for me is almost gone. Such is also the case for me with comic books. While I do still enjoy buying paper copies, I have gone probably at least eighty percent digital these days. It's just way easier, cheaper, and with services like Marvel Unlimited, I get four or more new comics every week I want to read.

Over the past few years, we decided to put security cameras in our house. While these are mainly just a way for us to check on our cats when we're away, one time they did provide us with some important knowledge. The ability to check on your house (and for us cats) from anywhere in the world, on your phone with the Internet for free is truly an amazing feat that I never would have thought possible just twenty years ago. Once when we were on vacation in Florida, I got a call late at night from our alarm company. Our alarm at our house back in Newfoundland was going off. This could have been a major problem but with our security cameras it was not. After checking all the cameras, we could see that no one had broken in and the cats were fine (if shook up by the alarm) and I told the security company to remotely turn off the alarm. Turns out it was so windy back home that a wire attached to one of the windows came loose, and the alarm went off. These fifty-dollar cameras saved us potentially thousands of dollars and gave us peace of mind knowing our house (and cats) were fine. I also must mention the ability to look up (and go to) any place in the world (walking, in a car, or on a bike) with Google Maps (or a similar app) is perhaps one of the greatest inventions I have ever seen. Yes, I'm aware you could get directions before with a GPS device (I had several) but just using an app on your phone is so much easier, it's certainly saved me hundreds of hours and allowed me to go to places I never would have otherwise.

I would be remiss if I did not talk about one of the worst ways ignorance is spread on the Internet, the phenomenon called 'infotainment' and 'misinformation'. Infotainment is when news is presented in an entertaining way, so not necessarily falsely, but in a fashion to keep your interest and watch through the commercials. A program like Entertainment Tonight would be considered infotainment and I have no problem with it, it is fashion/celebrity/entertainment news and will often be light in terms of subject matter. Even a paper like Weekly World News (which is now only online, it was on shelves until 2007) does not bother me because it is so obviously fake and can be funny (look up bat boy if you want a laugh). I used to look for this newspaper at the supermarket as it always made me smile and sometimes laugh out loud (though I never actually bought it).

The problem arises when you find an article that suggests strongly that COVID-19 was created in a lab (to the best of my knowledge this is not true). This article is done by two people who claim to have PhD's (if you believe it), has over half a million downloads and almost a million views. It looks like a real academic paper and so naturally would be taken as truth by many people who read it. This leads further credence to the conspiracy theory that the Chinese created the virus to take over, destroy, or destabilize the world. It has sadly created more racism, divide, and distrust of not only our fellow man (and woman) but also the government. The world is already a complicated, messy place that is increasingly full of violence, racism, and ignorance (especially this year). The thought of someone knowingly and intentionally making this worse is simply reprehensible. There is a site which disproves this article on COVID-19 as being intentional, but I only found it because I was actively looking for it, otherwise many people may accept the previous article as truth

To clue up, I think the Internet is an amazing tool, one that can be used for an incredible amount of good, fun entertainment, spreading of knowledge, making our lives easier, and connecting like-minded people. As with any tool, however, it has just as much potential to be used for much more malicious and negative things like the spreading of ignorance, increasing hate in the world, and sadly encouraging anti-social behavior. It can be tough to find the balance of what you should use the Internet for, it is part of our nature to want to taste forbidden fruit and I'll admit I've seen things on the Internet I wish I hadn't and there are sites I simply don't go to anymore.

I think that now more so than ever parents need to get involved with their children's lives. They need to monitor what they are doing on the Internet and possibly install something like Net Nanny if they feel it is necessary. Net Nanny is a program (or app for an iPhone) that controls what content someone can view on a tablet, phone or laptop in terms of appropriateness. So, if someone underage (and under your care) tried to look at pornography, Net Nanny would block that website (Riley, 2020). I can see how the Internet has changed the world in the past twenty years, how it made my life a lot easier and better in many ways, but I can also see the danger. I see how for something incredibly important like the US election how a foreign government can use the Internet to not only influence but to some extent rig an election (Mayer, 2018). I think it is true that Russia helped Trump win in 2016 and are attempting to do the same thing in 2020, all through the Internet (Barnes, 2021). I also see the benefits, how a social program like TikTok could be used by young people to make sure that a Trump rally had low attendance. I hope government officials, parents, industry leaders, and everyone else thinks about what they do on the Internet a little bit. Spend an extra minute thinking before you share a meme that could be offensive, think about a comment before you put in on someone's Facebook page, don't repost an article just because the headline says something you want to hear, the world is full of trickery and the Internet displays it more than anywhere else. If you are able, you should really fact check an article before you share it with other people. An easy way to do this is go to snopes.com and simply type in the title of your article, you'll then know it is a credible source. I hope in years to come the Internet will be used to make the world better, to help those who need it and bring light to important issues, I think if we all just make a little effort than it will be closer to reality. Just spend twenty minutes sometime and go through your Facebook friends, I would bet if there are over a hundred there is someone there who doesn't even like you and is only on to sell something or spread lies. I am an optimist but still realistic. I know the Internet isn't going anywhere but I can hope that good, creative people will find even better ways to use it and that all of us will benefit with a little more truth, positively, love, and friendship on our screens.

Chapter 9: Role-Playing Games

I have been playing role-playing (RP) for a long time, over thirty-two years as I write this, and it is something I still enjoy to this day. I wish I could tell you that I played as much as I did when I was a teenager or in my twenties (or hell, thirties) but that is not the case. Everyone grows up, lives get busy, people get jobs, move away, get married, have kids, get divorced, but for me RP has always been there and will always be something I dearly love. I've played at least twenty different systems ranging all the way from the one you may be familiar with: Dungeons & Dragons, to ones you've likely never heard of like Paranoia and Amber (which is a dice-less role-playing game, unusual). I have played characters from level one all the way up to fourteen and I've had characters die the first time I played them, but a lot of this may be gobbledygook to you, so I'll do some explaining.

I will assume that you do not know what a role-playing game (RPG) is and start from there. Explaining all the different mechanics, terms, slang, rules, themes, ideas, and systems would be a chapter onto itself, so I will just touch on it. We often hear the term role-play used in a sexual context for adults. What that means is that one (or both people) dress up in costume and/or take on a role, you pretend to be someone else, both of you act out a fantasy, it is a way for couples to spice up their relationship with something non-threatening and is often easy to do. Children do this in a non-sexual way when they dress up and play, even just with toys they are often acting out a story in their heads. The point is that you are pretending to be someone (or something) you are not, and you are in an imagined story where your actions matter and change the way it turns out. You can see how an RPG goes if you watch a particular episode of "The Big Bang Theory", to give a popular example. A more recent one would be the show "Stranger Things" on Netflix (a great show even if you do not care about RP), they feature D&D in several episodes and give a more accurate idea of what a game is a like than most TV shows I have seen. If you are looking for something more web-based there is also a series that shows full RP sessions (they are long videos!) called "Critical Role". Despite the three plus hour length to some of the videos they are entertaining and show what a RP session (for a D&D type game) is like.

For an RPG game you need supplies like dice (not just six-sided but many different varieties), a pencil, paper, and some rule books (though now you can get by with just the right apps on your phone). Some systems have their own dice, some have no dice at all, but either way you will have to read up on the game and be prepared. Let us stick with Dungeons & Dragons (D&D) as there's some chance you've heard of it (*The Lord of the Rings* books is what D&D was heavily based off).

To make your character, you follow instructions from the Player's Handbook, or GM/DM (Game Master/Dungeon Master) who runs the game. Here is where it gets interesting in that you have a huge number of choices of the type of character you want to play. You could be an elf ranger or elf fighter. You could be someone totally different like a dwarven wizard. The point is that this is a game that encourages you to use your imagination. While you can use miniatures (I have hundreds of them, which I used in the game and collect them) many don't. I use graph paper and have visual/audio/visual components, but you do not have to. At its heart an RPG is about someone telling a story and your character being a part of it. You have a character sheet in front of you which tells you about their abilities. Your character generally meets up with a group of other player characters (or PCs) in a fantasy world. If you're lucky it will be a group of friends, but you can certainly find comic book or hobby stores which have organized RPG nights for anyone interested (I have done this, and it can be fun). I'm lucky enough to have been playing with friends for over thirty years now (those people have changed of course but a few have been there since the start) and I have been in multiple RP groups, played at conventions, comic book stores, through message boards, online chat programs, Skype, and this year on Zoom. An RPG (with age-appropriate material of course) is a game that children should be encouraged to play. It not only helps with math (there is adding and subtracting numbers with the dice, and geography if using a map), it encourages socialization and turn-taking as you simply must talk to other people, you get the satisfaction of developing a character over time and as you grow up you can play with more serious ideas, situations, and themes. I think most importantly RP gets a child to use their imagination and takes them away from TV or videos games for at least a few hours.

Rather than discuss each article I will invite you to have a look at the references for this chapter. I think you will be both entertained and informed by the variety and scope of them. I was not popular in grade school, junior high, or high school. I was a huge nerd/geek (I think I am some combination of both as I love my hobbies and did well at school) and had a typical unpleasant experience. As such I had a strong desire to be a part of a group and to make friends. This was one of the reasons I got so heavily into RP. At first it was just three of us; myself and two of my oldest friends. As we got into high school however, we expanded and added other people to the group and eventually even women (lots of women RP now, but 30 years ago it was rarer). I would love to have more women role-play but, in my experience, most women don't have the same interest in it that men do (at least here in Newfoundland). Certainly, another important consideration is that for most of D&D's history all of the marketing was targeted towards men, so of course women felt left out and less inclined to play. Also, worth considering is that sadly a lot of men are total jerks and when a woman would RP they would make the experience so unpleasant for them that they would not come back. I think all those previously mentioned reasons along with (and as I was told by a female friend) that some women just don't have time for RP even if they have the interest. It's the difference between a high-maintenance and low-maintenance woman, it's always been obvious to me most women spend far longer on their appearance (and other grooming activities) than men do, that and of course when people have children RP must be put aside (at least partially) for several years. For a few years we had RP sessions constantly, once or twice a week every week for months on end, marathon sessions that went five, six, or even seven hours, and even whole weekends dedicated to RP (this eventually turned into a once-a-year activity that sadly ended a few years ago due to scheduling issues). All of this gave me a group where I belonged, it provided structure, and it provided me with something to look forward to, especially after a hard week at school or work.

People change and for a long time I really did not like to be alone, not for long periods of time anyway. I always wanted to be out every Saturday night, if I am being honest, I did not want too much time alone with my thoughts because I was sad or depressed a lot of the time. Thinking back now I realize I was just socially awkward and one of my major issues was that I had no idea how to approach, talk to, or ask out a woman and as time went by and I finished high school and entered my last semester at university (for my first degree) I started to feel I would always be alone. The other big issue for me was the bullying I was subjected to in high school. It was bad enough at the time, but I think the worst part is that the damage to my self-esteem lasted for years afterwards and I don't think it ever fully went away. Thankfully, I was wrong about finding a girlfriend, and I did meet someone just before I finished my Bachelor of Arts, but RP was like a long-time friend that stayed by my side.

RP has always been like a kind of emotional support system for me. For example, when I lost my job at a local trades college I did not wallow in failure, I had RP that night and it helped. As I said earlier, if on a Friday or Saturday night I did not have a date often I could have RP to look forward to. For me RP is a form of socializing and that means I will often have a drink (or many when I was younger) during a session. Obviously, I am not encouraging anyone to drink and like any activity for adults, I would say only have a drink if you are nineteen or older and enjoy it. To the best of my knowledge two of my friends do not drink alcohol (or take any kind of drug) and enjoy RP as much as I do, so it's certainly not a requirement and of course getting sloshed and RP is a bad idea.

I am lucky that we have always done a great variety of RPG over the years. I have always loved *Star Wars* (now more so than ever with all the great movies, TV shows, and comics) and I got to be in three different Star Wars RPG games. I should explain in this game it is not like you get to play Darth Vader and someone else is Luke Skywalker; that would just be crazy and take away all the challenges in the game. You are in the Star Wars world so while you could play a Wookie, you would not be Chewbacca, same goes for a droid, you could be a Protocol droid but not C3-PO. The fun part in the Star Wars RPG is that you do get to visit all the worlds you have seen in the movies, you will occasionally get a glimpse of Darth Vader over some Imperial transmission, and you will get to fight with the Rebellion and try to destroy the Empire just as you saw your favourite characters do on screen. While you will not be a Jedi you can (if you're not a droid) eventually learn to use the force and gain a few minor powers. One of the great thrills I got to have while playing a Star Wars game was holding (and turning on a lightsaber). I didn't know how to use it, hell I didn't even get to keep it, but it was still a blast. More recently Star Wars became important for me as we all coped with isolation, fear, and boredom during the worst of the pandemic here in Newfoundland. Having a Zoom Star Wars session every week was something I really looked forward to. It helped take my mind off the shitty world around me and brightened my spirits.

    I have always been a big horror fan too and it was (usually) a treat to play in a game called Call of Cthulhu (CoC). Cthulhu is a horror RPG that is based on the works by H.P. Lovecraft (a horror writer who died in 1937 but had a lasting impact on the genre) and is a lot different from D&D. While D&D is a fantasy game with all sorts of creatures, magic, and farfetched ideas (compared to the real world) CoC, on the other hand, is much more realistic in many ways. In CoC there is rarely magic healing for example. If your character gets shot, stabbed, mauled, or has any other grievous injury, they could die and would most certainly need to be hospitalized whenever possible. In CoC there is magic and there are monsters, but it is always hidden away, something regular people don't find out about or even if they do, they refuse to believe. Another important aspect to the game is that once your character dies, he or she stays dead (with a few notable exceptions), while in an RPG like D&D, death becomes less important as your characters advance in level and can do truly incredible feats such as massive healing or raising the dead. CoC is a horror game and has the interesting (and ultimately slightly depressing effect) of making all of your characters go insane, sooner or later. The idea in the game is that when you see something that is truly terrible, like a man suddenly sprouting a tentacle from his stomach that lashes out to grab you, your mind reels and you make this thing called a sanity check. Once you fail a sanity check (and eventually you will), you lose sanity and start to go insane. The concept being that if you make your check, you are in denial and don't see what happened as truly real but if you fail your check, your mind strains to accept that magic or monsters are real and in front of you! The idea being that if you encounter enough of the supernatural it corrupts your mind; it is just something human beings are not equipped to deal with. So, while at first you get phobias or complexes and act in completely irrational ways for periods of time, ultimately if your character doesn't retire, he or she ends up dead or committed to an asylum.

To give you an idea of the fun ideas a GM can come up with, I played a character who ended up alone during one adventure and was killed by a deranged scientist. Luckily for me however, this scientist was obsessed with raising the dead and he did so with me just when the other PCs showed up to confront him. As such I got play an undead character for many sessions (he was not a vampire, mummy, or even zombie in any traditional sense of those words). It was a lot of fun as he was tremendously strong and could take a lot of damage (in the game PCs have health which represents how many times they can be hurt without dying, they are often called hit points). The strain of being undead took its toll and he was slowly growing more violent and less capable of functioning at his job as a police officer. Eventually he had to be wrapped in bandages as his body started to fall apart from decay. He would talk to a psychiatrist all the time (one of the other PCs was one) but she eventually could no longer treat him to due to the state of his insanity. In the end he died in a fist fight with a mummy who literally beat him to death. It remains an example of the GM doing a great job of coming up with a clever idea for a PC, rather than just having him or her die and create a new one. I am lucky to have had several excellent GMs who have done lots of great sessions and games. With one, what I really admire about his style is that it has changed, matured over the years, and only gotten better. We started off playing D&D and I had fun things happen to a character like becoming a bear. This was not just for a session; this was for months, and I embraced it. You would be surprised how much fun you can have doing something as simple as playing a bear when you use your imagination (a player in the group was a Ranger, which means he could communicate with me, and I could thus communicate with everyone else). As the years went by, the GM developed stories that touched on TV shows I loved, ones people from outside of Newfoundland most likely had never heard of like *Pigeon Inlet*. He gave me the chance to play characters I loved from more well-known TV shows like Michael Knight (*Knight Rider*) and Super Dave Osborne (from *Bizarre*).

His ability to come up with unique ideas that appealed to what the players wanted and challenged them (both in terms of playing different roles and learning history) is a fantastic combination and something I always love to do. I can honestly say that his sessions are the ones where I have laughed, had the most fun, and felt the most challenged intellectually. Through the years and hundreds of sessions he has also pulled the most on my nostalgic heart strings and showed the most effort to put a little something into a story that all of us would enjoy and connect with.

I have also been a GM for a quite a long time and have a little to say about my many experiences and what they mean to me. I will admit right away that I used to be a terrible GM. I just used it to indulge in all the things I wanted to do and explore crazy ideas I had. I even took a break from running D&D (which I have done probably nine out of ten times) to do this terrible game called Star Fleet Battles (which is an official *Star Trek* product). The game was really it was just a way to simulate space battles, with no characters or anything like it. The rules were so complex that I re-wrote and simplified them for my friends. When I think about the time I devoted to role-playing, to be a better GM I would read rule books from cover to cover. I would go over frequently asked questions (FAQ) on the rules whenever there was an update. I spent thousands of dollars and hundreds of hours buying, categorizing, and then finding ways to use miniatures (still do buy them but have slowed down tremendously). But I do love my collection, it is really the only thing I collect anymore.

Suffice it to say that if you have an obsessive personality (which I certainly do), it is easy to become heavily involved with the business of being a GM. As time passed however, I grew and became a better storyteller, I listened to my players when they did not like something, and I became a better GM. When I GM I make it a combination of available published adventures and my own stories. As such, I found I was creating character arcs, coming up with large world events, tying together stories in a large world fabric, showing character development with non-player characters (NPCs) and generally just imagining stuff all the time. I think it is no coincidence that my favorite part of the D&D game (both as a player and as a GM) is the combat, and when I later got serious about writing I discovered it was combat scenes I loved to write the most. Being a GM also means a lot to me personally, it was also something fun to do when I was lonely and bored.

While I have played with strangers and people I would consider just casual acquaintances, I will say that playing (or running) an RPG with friends you've known for years certainly makes for the more enjoyable experience. Being a GM is more work than being a player; it means more planning and reading, but it is also more rewarding. I have had some great moments as a GM where characters who were supposed to be really hated or loved by the players, got the reactions I wanted! I have gotten to describe scenes that I spent months planning, and seen them turn into exciting moments, and I've elicited instances of genuine surprise and delight from players that made all the work worth it. For someone who generally loves to plan, being a GM for the most part is something I enjoy, and it is almost always worth it for me. I love it when my friends show up for an RP session that I'm running. I know I'm prepared and I'm always a little excited to see how my plans will turn out. Overall, the players I've had over the years have been creative, surprising, and always make the game more fun and interesting. With that same token players have also quickly spotted short cuts I might have missed in a story or combat; they always think of better ways to use combat abilities than I ever did, and keep me honest. They certainly show the flaws in a game and give you plenty of hints when sometimes a particular campaign just becomes broken, and you must let it die.

RPG is an important part of my life and will continue to be for as long as I can manage. They have showed me what true friends look like. It has been a social activity, a source of relaxation, a creative fuel and drive, a chance to learn more of history and literature, to be exposed to different kinds of music, culture, and an avenue to allow players to interact with different people. For me RP is almost part of the fabric of who I am. I genuinely do not feel like myself if I must go a month or more without RP of some kind. While I will admit that my love for it is probably not the norm, I am convinced that anyone who is introduced the right way (with a story/setting they are interested in, and friendly and helpful people), can grow to like it. I think everyone could benefit from a little role-playing even it is just going to a murder mystery party, putting on a mask in the bedroom, or even just being a part of a child's make-believe for a little while. As children we love to dress-up, our imagination is in its purest form and is eager to grow. Most people give up these fun activities when it seems childish, and they put that part of themselves away. When you continue to do RPG, however, it is a like a part of your mind never fully grows up. You manage to keep a little childlike spark of wonder, even if it is only for a few hours during a session of gameplay.

We all have dark thoughts, moments of weakness, things we wish we never said or did. All these things can lead to huge problems if acted on but if you just do something in an RPG it's not real, it doesn't affect you or anyone else. That is one of the truly fantastic benefits, you can act out a fantasy and there is no real-life consequence. You work through things in your mind, can get your aggression out in a healthy way, and doesn't lead to broken bones or furniture. I think more-so these days than ever, the world can be a miserable place. So why not spend time with other people and imagine how different it could be? Why not encourage your friends in a cooperative game that will make you all closer as human beings? It's hard to imagine a more worthwhile activity you can do with your clothes on.

Chapter 10: Cycling

I do not claim to be any kind of athlete. In fact, I had a big wakeup call this year when I went to a dietician, was weighed and told that technically my body fat analysis (a machine I stood on did this along with a computer) indicated I was obese. I have almost always been a little heavy, I like to eat and drink, and, in the winter, I get less exercise. As I have gotten older, I have grown to hate the cold winter months here in Newfoundland even more and it has become a real effort to exercise outside or indoors during those months. When I was given this diagnosis, I had been exercising for months and had already lost weight but still it stung and hurt my self-esteem. Cycling is, for most people I think in North America at least, something they start doing as a child. Learning to ride a bike is a part of growing up. We have all heard expressions like "You never forget, it's like riding a bike!" and there is lots of proof that our bodies have muscle memory which never goes away. So, like millions of other kids, I learned to ride a bike and I loved it.

When I was young there were not many good trails around my house, and I went on the road. When I got to be a teenager I even went on the highway (which I see now was dangerous and I should not have done so). I would ride from our house (in Manuels, Conception Bay South) and go all the way to my grandmother's house (who lived in St. John's a good distance, about twenty-four kilometers away). It would take hours for me to do it (I'd always go with a friend) and it would be an adventure. We'd be tired and thirsty, and my grandmother would bring us food and refreshments when we got there. My mom or dad would come in a van to pick us up (as I did not have the energy to ride back home again) and it used to make me feel great. I remember when I would get ahead of my friend on the highway and would sing to myself a song by Alphaville called *Forever Young*. Getting to the home stretch of the ride and singing that song was a great feeling. The song is about the loss of youth and the meaning of life but back then I was just celebrating being young.

Also, like lots of people, I lost interest in cycling when I got my license and got a car (I had one when I was seventeen, I was lucky, and fortunate with a lot of things in my life). It is weird how you just forget about something and years later it comes back to you. For a long time, I never even thought of riding a bike (over fifteen years) and then my wife bought us both bikes and we used them but only sporadically. Eventually the bikes got put away, got dusty, and were forgotten about in our basement.

More time passed and we moved from Cherry Lane to a new subdivision. During the move I thought about throwing the bikes out (or selling them), but my wife convinced me not to. In our new house we live right on a walking trail (which people also ride bikes on) and decided it was time to give cycling another try. I will say that my wife was certainly right, and I was thrilled to rediscover my love of cycling. I planned it when we bought the land to be on an extensive trail network where I can ride my bike for a long time (over 25 kilometers in one direction) and pass-through woods, go by farms, streams and the ocean. The other way is more challenging (as I head towards Paradise) as the trail eventually gets rough ungroomed and narrow but does eventually come out by a nice pond to ride around where I can feed the ducks and can usually avoid traffic.

There is no doubt that cycling is good for your body, and I am happy to say that this summer with a lot of cycling (and an improvement to my diet) I lost fourteen pounds and feel a whole lot better about myself. It uses your legs a lot but with turning and stabilizing is also good workout for your upper body. There is a good website (Betterhealth, 2020) which the government of Victoria, Australia made that talks about how it can help you lose fat, build muscle, strengthen bones, reduce your chances of having a stroke, heart problems and high blood pressure. If that was not enough, some studies show it can prevent certain kinds of cancers and helps with anxiety and depression. I can say personally that this year I have truly come to love cycling, so much that for the first time ever I rented a bike while I was on vacation and am now planning future trips with the intent of finding biking trails near where we are staying.

I made a promise to myself in May that I was going to push myself, to get on the bike even if it was a little rainy, windy, or cold (in Newfoundland we get that a lot, to some extent year-round) and I would ride more and further than I ever had before. I am happy to say that I kept that promise (not necessarily every day and some weeks I did better than others). I have a routine that I kept to. I tried to get in a forty-five to one-hour bike ride at least three days a week before work and on the weekends at least one day I push myself hard and do anywhere from an hour and half to three hours of riding. I found a great app (free) that could track how far I went, the time it took, how many calories I burned, and other useful info. I should say that I do not push myself in terms of how fast I go, three hours for me is leisurely as I take breaks to eat, drink water, send texts, and sometimes just sit and meditate.

While the health benefits are great, it is important for me that it also helps me mentally. This year (2020) has been a rough one for us all and I have been more stressed than usual. I find that the fresh air and exercise helps me to calm down and find some happiness. Riding my bike in the morning (usually) puts me in a better mood for the whole day. It is a combination of things for me; I love to look at the water and I can be near the water after about fifteen minutes of riding from my house. Then I get to look at the ocean while I ride for an hour or so, and on a nice day when the trail is not too crowded it can be a wonderful experience. I have a listening schedule; usually I start out with some music (I have specific playlists for Newfoundland, summer, travel and other things) then listen to an audio book, then usually for the last bit some music again. While I could hardly be called an adrenaline junkie, I do enjoy the feeling of going fast and while that is unsafe in a car, on a bike it's just fine. Going downhill as fast as I can while listening to some of my favorite songs (give a listen to *Love Becomes Electric* by Strange Advance sometime) can be sheer euphoria.

Cycling also leads me to wonderful moments of quiet contemplation, mediation of a sort. It's a time when I just sit on my bike, have a drink of water or a snack, and look out at the ocean. I take in these moments when there is no one else around and it is just me, my bike, and the sound of the waves or the distant sound of birds. Several times I have gone for a ride and there have been cats wandering around the trail, also chickens (I go past several farms), rabbits, and goats (they were tied on but still on the trail on occasion). I love animals and this always brought a smile to my face. Moments I have on the trail help to quiet my mind, give me an appreciation for the beauty around me, helps me keep things in perspective and makes me wonder about the future. We do not plan to be in Newfoundland for the rest of our lives, as much as I love this province. I have a deep desire to travel. You feel more of a connection with the community as I get to see the same people many days (not that I know their names, but I wave and say "Hello!") and I find it a comfort to see them on a regular basis. I am the kind of person that likes routine and when I see people, places, and animals that are familiar to me on a regular basis, it helps me stay focused and I enjoy the structure in my life.

As I have said while I love to listen to music, I also quite enjoy listening to audio books. It is wonderful to lose yourself in a book while you are outside cycling, it gives you more time to imagine what you're listening to and I can even remember where I was outside when I was listening to a specific part of a book written by Bruce Springsteen. I love to associate places with certain memories and ideas. It is funny how if you do something enough (and you truly enjoy it), it becomes a part of who you are. I am going to give you a few examples of how much I've come to love cycling and how it's changed my life. I used to be a person who got up on a Saturday or Sunday (often both) and would spend at least two hours watching TV (or a movie) while eating popcorn. I used to love this and really looked forward to it every weekend. On this one Sunday however, after an hour or so sitting outside I realized I just could not just sit there. It was just too nice a day, and I knew I would regret it if I did not hop on my bike and get moving, so I did.

Another night (a Friday) I was at a friend's house to play some board games. I had not seen this friend in years, and I was having a good time. As the hours wore on however, I made it known that I would not be staying later than ten. I just explained that I loved to get up on a Saturday (the forecast was good for the next day) and ride for hours and I knew if I stayed up late, I would sleep in and it just wouldn't be as good. I think he was surprised and maybe even a little annoyed at me, but I stuck to my guns, I came and stayed for over three hours and my weekend cycling just meant too much to me to miss. Another good example is this fall when I decided I wanted to get some liquor for the weekend. I was driving back from getting a massage and for a second, I thought I could just continue and drive to the liquor store but in my mind, something tugged at me, I didn't need to drive. I am lucky that I can ride my bike from my house and be at a liquor store and supermarket within twenty minutes. This was a cold, rainy, dull day but I knew it would be better for me, the environment, and ultimately put me in a better mood for the evening, so I did it. Not only did I ride to get my booze, but I was enjoying myself enough that I continued out and ended up being gone for about an hour and half. I am the kind of person that hates the rain, cold, wind, fog and basically only likes warm, sunny, calm weather. Riding my bike on rainy days (or even walking) was something I would not have done four years ago, but this year I did it with only a few seconds of hesitation. I think that says a lot about what regular cycling did for me and what I think it could do for you.

Cycling is not just about the mental and physical aspects; you start to feel a connection with your bike. I've had mine long enough and put in enough hours riding it that when a guy at the bike shop told me I'm too big for it and I need a new one, I felt disappointment and sad that I wouldn't' be doing it this year. This year I invested in the bike and in gear such as riding shorts, gloves, a long-sleeved exercise shirt and cycle leggings. I bought a new seat, new handlebar grips and spent money getting the bike serviced twice (once for the yearly tune-up and once for a flat tire, breaks and the gears). I did research on how high the seat should be, where the handlebars should be and what posture you should have while riding. I sometimes pick out certain albums to listen to when I am riding (often live concerts) and won't finish my ride until I'm through the whole thing.

I even have an attachment that turns my outdoor bike into an indoor exercise one (which I am sadly going to need this weekend as it's November here in Newfoundland) and use it all winter long until I can go outside again. In 2019 I waited until mid-June before I got on my bike outside (as it's just damn cold here until then) but this year I was glad I pushed myself and started a full month before that, braving lots of cold days on the bike in May, June, and even July. One day I went out despite the cold and rain for over two hours because I didn't want to break my routine of a long ride on a Saturday. I've discovered that getting cold and wet doesn't make you sick and I'd argue that outdoor exercise (within limits), helps you fight off any infection as it boosts your immune system (I would not go out in an ice storm, snowstorm, or rainstorm of course). My family doctor told me that anytime you can force your body to deep breathe you should and that outdoor exercise (especially here in Newfoundland where we have no smog and little pollution) is so much better than being inside.

I would encourage anyone who is able to ride a bike to do so. Start small, do what you can do it terms of time, distance, hills and keep going. It is a unique experience as it forces you to concentrate on the road or trail for stretches but also leaves you plenty of time to think, look around, and connect with nature (assuming you are not just riding on the roads—I'm lucky to have plenty of nature trails around me). It is a weird thing that we often think of riding a bike as being something just for kids when that is not the case at all. I enjoyed riding a bike when I was young but now that I really need the exercise, clarity, stress-relief, and time to myself, I enjoy it much more than I ever did. So, get a used bike (or a new one if you can), find a place you'd like to ride and get out there. I ride by myself but if having a buddy to ride with is better for you, then do it. Do not worry about what anyone thinks of you or how well you do. Follow your local safety regulations and just get on your bike and ride, you will be glad you did.

Chapter 11: Musical Medicine

I have always loved music. For as long as I can remember it's been an important part of my life. I mean really, who does not love music? I cannot imagine a culture where songs or music doesn't hold an important part of everyone's lives. As an interesting aside, Amish people are not allowed to listen to music (any kind of recording) but sing all the time. The article I read said many people do up to two hours a day! So, while they don't listen to it on their iPhones, they certainly enjoy it none the less and it is an important part of their society (Nussbaum, 2002). I don't come from a musical family, my mom can play a little piano (by ear, she doesn't read music) but I think it was more my dad who most shaped the way I feel about music. I think it was him playing music from the 60s, 70s and 80s that most influenced what kind of music I love today. He used to help me fall asleep when I was a baby by playing *Lyin' Eyes* by The Eagles. I dearly love that song and I even had it play during our wedding.

I remember how excited I was to first get a Walkman (it is a primitive device compared to what we have now, which could play just one album at a time on cassette tapes). To me it was a wonder. As I discussed in Chapter 10, I loved to ride my bike and when I was, 10 or 11 the ability to ride my bike around while listening to music was a slice of heaven. I would listen to top hits from 1984, '85 and '86 as I rode my bike for hours around our house (we had a fair bit of land and a long driveway). I grew up listening to people like Corey Hart, Eurythmics, The Payolas, Duran Duran and Platinum Blonde just to name a few. As soon as I was able to, I started asking my parents to take me to concerts. While listening to a song on the radio or on tape was good, it held no comparison to seeing a band or singer in person. I am not exactly sure who I saw at my first concert, but I know which ones made an impression.

Huey Lewis and the News were an early one for me. This concert was at the old Memorial Stadium (which later became a supermarket). They are certainly an '80s band with their peak being 1985 and "The Power of Love" (from *Back to the Future* of course! A movie I love to this day). Seeing a movie and then hearing the title song performed was a thrill for me, it is still something I quite enjoy and even though I remember having terrible seats (we were behind a large steel beam). I loved them so much that when I had a chance some thirty years later, I got to see them again at our newer stadium, Mile One. I was lucky that my parents took me to lots of concerts I wanted to see including Chris De Burgh, Glass Tiger, The Guess Who, The Beach Boys and other shows when I was an adult and we decided to go together.

I loved music so much that I would take cassettes (and later CDs) and mark them up in the order of personal preference rather than the numerical order. I used to carry around a case of cassettes whenever I was on any kind of trip or even going over to see a friend or family member. Cassettes were a big deal for music, it meant you could record songs off the radio, get a lousy quality version of a song from a movie on TV (or VHS! If you know what either of those things are you must be forty or close to it) or with a little ingenuity (and by that, I mean scotch tape in the right spots) you could make a copy of someone else's cassette. I remember holding onto cassettes for a long time. I can't say for sure, but I think I had my first CD player somewhere around 1989 (they came out in 1983 but cost a fortune back then).

Music has changed a lot in various formats, and I haven't bought a CD in years (I'd say ten or more), but I did keep a lot of them, and I remember them fondly. Just watching them spin around was always enjoyable for me. Now we have MP3s (digital files of songs) and personally I listen to all my music through Amazon Music, and only occasionally listen to the radio or sometimes YouTube for more obscure songs.

The first band I really loved and made a point to follow (and yes eventually see in concert) was the Eurythmics. Their biggest hit was "Sweet Dreams (Are Made of This)" which came out in 1984, so it's entirely possible you've never heard them before. I remember first hearing "Sweet Dreams (Are Made of This)" on a hit collection (tape) from 1984. Something drew me to their music, and I started buying their albums. By 1999 I had every album they had released (including a few I had to order away for). I even went so far as to find some of the Extended Plays (EP) (that means albums with just a few songs on it, I do not know if they're even made anymore) and bought some mix CDs off a guy on the Internet. These mixed CDs had Eurythmics songs I had never heard before and different versions of other songs I loved. For years this meant I would also collect everything I could find by Dave Stewart and Annie Lennox (while the Eurythmics are a band, these are the only two permanent members). Even if you don't like the Eurythmics I would encourage you to listen to one song by Annie Lennox called "Pavement Cracks"; her voice is truly incredible. She would also win an Academy Award for "Into the West" (from *The Lord of the Rings: The Fellowship of the Rings* soundtrack), which is also a great song well worth a listen.

They were the first band whose lyrics spoke to me and that I made a connection with. For me music leads me to do things I would not have otherwise. For example, with the Eurythmics, I loved them so much that a friend and I went to see them in New York City (NYC). Not only that but because I was part of e-mail group, I also met a whole bunch of people at a restaurant NYC, something I had never done before. Music has changed me as a person, made me more outgoing and got me to travel to many places to see concerts. I am the type of guy who will go to up to a singer at a bar (or restaurant) and make a request (with a tip for them of course). If I did not love music (and in particular wanting to hear my own specific songs) I know I would be much less outgoing. I saw The Rolling Stones on my birthday one year in Toronto (excellent show, Mick still had the moves like Jagger!) as a birthday present from my wife. While at the Stones concert a guy (and a woman) just started talking to me. I had on a Stones shirt and was in a good mood, so the three of us chatted about the band, their songs, and how great they were for a good five minutes before the show started. It is something I have always felt is so great about music; it brings people together and gives them something they can all enjoy, even if only for a few hours at a show.

A good song is poetry put to music and in it you can always find some words of wisdom or something that makes your life a little clearer. I had a hard time in high school. I was a nerd or geek and got picked on. I am sure other kids had it worse, but it left a lasting, negative impression and I really hated school. There is a song called "Thorn in my Side" and for a long time for me it was like high school and all the people there I hated; I felt such relief to be finally finished there in '94. The Eurythmics do have some sad songs but overall, their music is positive, and it helped me through some tough times. I was giddy with excitement when I got to buy a new album from them in '89 (*We Too Are One*) and of course their final non-compilation album in '99 called *Peace,* which is excellent and raises lots of important issues about the world.

I have been to concerts in lots of different places, have seen some people multiple times (I think Blue Rodeo is the most for me—at least six times) and I am also happy to say that I got to see The Eagles while Glenn Fry was still alive. I also enjoy some local music and saw Ron Hynes several times before he died as well. While the concerts I went to in the USA were certainly bigger in terms of crowd size than anything in Canada, I also enjoyed the smaller shows more. I loved Ron Hynes' music and seeing him in a bar (a small bar here in Newfoundland called The Fat Cat) was a wonderful night. If you ever want to hear some excellent folk or soft rock music, I would highly recommend Ron Hynes, his signature song is "Sonny's Dream" and it certainly holds a lot of meaning for many people from Newfoundland (and I am sure many others from small towns).

When I was nine or ten for some reason, I decided I wanted to learn to play the flute. My parents bought one for me and enrolled me in lessons. I think they only lasted for a few months as the instructor finally had to tell my mom that I was not any good at it and had the wrong shaped mouth. At the time I remember not enjoying it, so it really didn't bother me to stop. Years later (when I was 22) I decided to try learning piano. We always had a piano in the house so I certainly had access to it and appreciated how nice a song could be. I remember a friend of mine, Rhodi, would be at the house and he would play piano. He was excellent, he did an amazing job on "November Rain" by Guns 'N' Roses and it certainly inspired me to learn how. So, by the time I was twenty-three I had been taking lessons for a while. I learned the scales, how to read music, and how to play some basic songs. I really liked my instructor and when he left the music school I went to; I followed him and took lessons out of his house.

I will not dwell on my piano playing too long, it was a period of my life that I really enjoyed, picking out new songs to learn, getting better with them, discovering what I could and could not do. I soon learned I really could not do anything approaching a fast song and to get a song even close to sounding good I had to practice a lot. Some of the songs I could do okay on were "Piano Man" by Billy Joel, "Hey Jude" by The Beatles and "Imagine" by John Lennon. When I moved out of my parents' house, I was lucky to be given my grandmother's piano and spent many hours playing on it. Eventually my piano instructor became a full-time minister, and he did not have time to teach me anymore. Without Chris I lost my enthusiasm to play, and I just stopped playing. Right now, in my office I am looking at some of the lyrics to "Imagine" by John Lennon. I don't see how anyone can deny it's a beautiful song full of meaning. Lennon was a little extreme sometimes sure, but his message of peace, understanding, and acceptance is more important now than ever. One of the biggest issues we have in the world now is fear of other people or cultures. We focus on how we are different when it just does not matter. We are all human beings trying to find some happiness in the world. I think if everyone just took a moment to realize that we have more in common with any other person than there are differences, the world would be a much nicer, more peaceful place. I just cannot pick a song by The Beatles; I love them, and they changed music forever, but I do not know what song they did that best speaks to the human condition. Whatever your favorite is, listen to it closely and hopefully you can find meaning in the words.

    Another song which really speaks to me is "For a Dancer" by Jackson Brown. It is a rough one, people think it is about his girlfriend who died but it is about the loss of his friend. While the song is sad, there are still some wonderful lines from it about making the most of life and trying to find happiness. I think for me it really helps put everything in perspective. You must accept that no matter how wonderful, mediocre, or even shitty your life is that it is finite. You can be a Nobel Prize winner or the richest person in the world but either way you will have to face death and grapple with what you did with your life. I suppose this book is also about the most profound questions we ever face, what is the meaning of life? What can we do to give our lives purpose? I can't give any final answer of course but I think this song suggests that ultimately, we can't be too concerned with it.

The world just gets more complicated and confusing every day it seems and there isn't a person alive who has all the answers. Also, personally I think this is a perfect song to play at a funeral, remembrance, or celebration of life event. I plan to do a celebration of life (which means you kind of have a living wake) and this will certainly be a song I play. I want to hear people's reactions to my choices of music. While it might be a little grim the next song is also about the meaning of life and the end of it.

There was a wonderful band that only put out two albums called The Traveling Wilburys. I will admit right away that I only ever listened to the first one, since Roy Orbison died before the second one was started. The first album won all kinds of awards, sold very well, and is still played on lots of oldies and classic rock stations today. It has a wonderful song on it called "End of the Line." This is a song that deals with death and the acceptance of it, but it is also full of lessons and tips for living your life. It talks about truth that money, no matter how much you have, cannot buy you happiness. It talks about how important forgiveness is. If you hold onto hate it will consume you, I know that sounds like something Yoda would say but it is true, people full of hate only hurt others and destroy themselves. It talks about how getting old is not so bad, ultimately what becomes most important (beyond basic mobility and use of our motor functions) is the brain. I would be content if I end up in my 80s and cannot do strenuous exercise anymore. Our minds are the greatest gift we will ever have and if I can hold onto that, I know I can be happy in life. The song ultimately says (and I agree) that if you are happy and not hurting anyone, then that is really all you can ask for in life. How you achieve that happiness is, of course, different for each person and will always be a lifelong pursuit.

Another song which has come to mean a great deal to me is "Like a Rock" by Bob Seger. I know what your first thought might be (if you're old enough to remember), 'Seriously! You mean the song used for the Chevy Truck commercials? That is so cliché and he was a sellout!' A lot of people thought that Seger either wrote that song for the commercial or he was paid by Chevrolet to use it, but neither is true. Seger gave them the song to use for free because a car manufacturing plant (a Chevrolet one, of course) is in his hometown and he wanted it to do well. That is just some trivia though. This song is really a triple-whammy for me. As I have said I continue to love music from the '80s and this came out in 1986. I was twelve and really started enjoying buying my own music and discovering what I really liked.

The song just takes me back instantly to a summer in Eastport (a small town here in Newfoundland, one of the few with a sandy beach). We would have family vacations there all the time in the summer and I have a lot of good memories from those days. So, this song was playing, it was a warm summer night, and I was sitting on a picnic table playing with my toys. Let us be specific, because it really matters; they were Rock Lords (creatures that transformed into rocks). How exciting is that? So, I am playing with Rock Lords, the song "Like a Rock" is on the radio and my dad says "Hey listen! They're singing about your toys!" At the time it made me a little mad but now I see it was funny. So now as my dad has passed a few years ago, it becomes this bittersweet memory all tied up in the song. The song reminds us that truly the most special thing we can do is remember the best days of our lives and hope that those good ones will always outnumber the bad.

Music is such a personal thing that I acknowledge that a song I love could easily be one you hate; I am picky as I grew up listening to '70s and '80s music. As such, I find anything in the '90s suspect and from 2000 on there's little chance that I will like it. I suppose you might say I am in a little bit of musical rut, but I keep discovering (re-discovering) artists I love from the '70s, '80s (and yes a few from the '90s). I just don't see much reason to try to discover new artists (that said occasionally I do, I enjoy The Weeknd and even plan to see him in concert in Amsterdam). Music for me is often a comfort. I want to remember how I felt in 1986 or 1994. I read an article about music and memory (Jenkins, 2014) and it really is true how a song can bring you right back to when you first heard it.

I think that no matter how I am feeling, there is a song that will nail it. For example, if I am feeling down (as certainly happened in 2020 and 2021 during the worst of the pandemic), I listen to "Wild Child" by Enya and feel a bit better. While it is slow and mellow, I strongly encourage you to give it a listen. The song talks about how the struggle to find meaning can make you less happy. Some days you get a lot done, feel accomplished and satisfied but others you just don't. Some days it is all you can do just to go to work, come home, watch some TV (or read perhaps) and call it a night—and that is fine, that's the way life is. Life goes on, spring, summer, fall and winter come and go, and you need to find a way to just be happy with the way the world (and you own life) is. Many people fall into a trap of always wanting more when one of the important lessons you learn in life is to be happy with what you already have. While I used to make mix CDs (and mix tapes) I find it much easier now to make a playlist with Amazon Music for certain occasions. For example, I made a specific mix for riding my bike outside, some of the songs mention bike riding but mostly they are just a collection of songs I love that flow well together.

    I would say that no matter what you do (or like to do in your free time) you need to spend more of it listening to music. It will continue to delight you and one of the best parts is that you can find as much enjoyment from discovering a new song you like as you do relistening to a song you have loved for many years. Not to sound too new-age but I do believe that music is one of the few things that can unite many people. Music is full of universal themes and until we have a full functional *Star Trek* universal translator, is the only universal language. Music will always mean a tremendous deal to me, and it is when you think about it, the soundtrack to your life. I hope that music does (or someday will) mean a lot to you. It remains one of the cheapest (and easiest) ways to find a little more happiness, excitement, introspection or whatever emotion you're feeling turned up a notch. Music can be one of the purest and most direct forms of communication from an artist to a listener and it is one I'll hold tight to for the rest of my life.

Chapter 12: Relationships

I used to be shy, painfully so. I did not like calling people on the phone or going into stores. I basically made efforts to avoid human contact and I suffered the consequences. For a long time (into my early twenties) I was lonely, felt disconnected from the world, and that I did not belong anywhere (aside from with my group of friends). I'm not going to get into some kind of psycho-self-analytical tangent, I know that my experiences in school (a lot of them negative and painful) had a major effect on me and I know also that it had to do with my personality (I can be bossy and rigid in my ideas, but I've gotten a bit better). The point I am making was that for me I wanted to experience a closeness with someone. I wanted a girlfriend and until I found one there was a loneliness in me that just never went away. Don't get me wrong, I've always had friends, my parents showed me love and affection (along with family members) but none of those things can compare with the love, physical connection, and closeness you can find with someone you truly love and who loves you back. I think all of us experience love at (hopefully) mainly points in their lives but not everyone gets to truly experience being in love. Before I go any further, I'll state the obvious; while I feel you will be a happier, more complete person with a spouse (and there is research to support this), I know there are people happy by themselves. To the best of my knowledge my great aunt, who lived to be over 90, never married (or even had a boyfriend) and was happy her whole life. So, if you're happy by yourself, then do not feel pressured to find someone, we are all different and I firmly believe if you are happy and not hurting anyone, then you have done what is most important for you. I have changed my feelings on relationships a lot over the years. When I was in my early twenties, I really felt the need to make new friends, to not spend much time by myself, and of course to end my long quest to find a girlfriend. I was (and to a much lesser extent still am) the person who was always planning social gatherings, movies, dinners, walks, and any other activities to keep from being alone.

I used to have this strange idea that it was terrible to go to a movie by yourself. I suppose somehow, I felt it was a little pathetic if you could not get anyone go to with you. I realized now just how silly I was, while I think going to a movie is a shared experience, going by yourself is a fine way to do it. The only thing I would add is that when you see a movie you really love (or even really hate), it is nice to get the feedback from another person instantly and have a quick discussion as you leave the theater. When you think about it, friendships are work, especially if the person moves away. I think that I realized as I got older that ultimately when you are around people all the time you just see their flaws more; they start to get on your nerves. Of course, I know I do the same, we are all flawed human beings, and it is frankly amazing that anyone can spend long periods of time and maintain long-lasting relationships with other people. There is a show called "The I.T. Crowd" (you really need to watch if you never have). In one episode there is a line that rings true, "People, what a bunch of bastards!" It's meant to be funny and not taken literally of course but when you think about it, it holds wisdom. The more people you meet and interact with, the more chances you will come across people you really do not like. I believe the world is full of mostly good people but there are a lot of bastards and unless you are a true hermit, you are going to run into them from time to time. There is a saying that among every group of friends there is a person no one likes and if you do not know who that person is, then it is you! So, it means I have the greatest respect for anyone who deals with the general public daily, it takes a lot of patience, and you deal with a lot of jerks. I do not want this chapter to be about the negative, though. What I am saying is that if you can, weed out the people who are just causing you grief and you really do not enjoy spending time with. There are a few people I have cut out of my life or at least reduced the amount of time I see them, and I am happier because of it. We live in strange times and the definition of a friend or relationship is changing. Is someone you only see on Zoom a friend? What about a Facebook friend? An Instagram follower? I have met people I spoke to on the Internet but most of them I would not consider friends, perhaps casual acquaintances. What about people you work with? My work is unusual as I work with my wife, brother, and sister-in-law but aside from those people I would not consider any of the staff as friends. I think it has to do with working with people Monday to Friday (and sometimes for me evenings and weekends). You see plenty of them, so the idea of seeing them again outside of work is often not appealing. I think I have a good core group of friends, many of whom I have known a long time (some over forty years!) and a few who are newer as friends of mine get divorced, meet new people and then get re-married.

Life is weird; when I was younger, I hated the thought of another Friday and Saturday night alone. But then when I got a girlfriend (or spouse) and got married we are together all the time. Naturally as years pass you miss having time to yourself and you come to look forward to the occasional night, weekend, or even short trip by yourself. With my friends what happened (and I think this is the case for a lot of people) your friends get divided into people who do and do not have children. We did not have children and as such we tended to spend more time with people who also are childless. This naturally meant I would see less of friends who did have children, as they are just a lot busier.

Speaking of children, when I ponder it, I can easily see how my relationship with my parents changed as I grew up. When you are a child you (generally) accept your parent's authority, you look up to them and you look to them for guidance and advice. As you get older you become an adult and the desire to live with your parents lessens as you want to make your own decisions and live your life differently from theirs. I can only speak from my perspective; I am aware some people live with their parents into their thirties and forties but for me the relationship had to change, and I was glad to move out at twenty-three.

I think this past year has forced millions of people to learn how to be happy by themselves or at least with less people in their lives. I never thought I would be having a trivia night over Zoom but such are the times we live in. I can say that because of the pandemic I see (in-person) all my friends a lot less than I did before, and I do miss the regular social get-togethers we had. I have had more time than ever before to think and reflect on life, to build a closer relationship with myself and with my wife, and I wonder if things will ever go back to the way they were. For example, we have our role-playing sessions now over Zoom and I have to say the convenience is wonderful, not having to leave the house, being able to get a bit tipsy and not concern myself with how I will get home, two major pluses. One group I dearly miss. We would play every week (with breaks of course when not enough people were free, or something came up) and have supper before the game started. It is something that is ingrained in North American culture for people to share meals together; it makes us more social somehow. I just do not feel the same closeness when we play over Zoom. They are all still close friends of course but I have not seen either group in person in almost a year now and it just makes me a little sad. I hope that when the pandemic finally ends, we can get together like we used to, even if only once a month perhaps.

It is interesting when you think about how relationships are defined, there are people I only see at work, others I only see at conventions, still others only for poker games and of course family you only see for birthdays, holidays or other occasional gatherings. For me there were even people (holiday friends) I would only see on holiday as we had a house in Florida for many years. I have always had a limit when it came to family gatherings. For example, during Christmas functions for years after supper I would sneak up to my cousins' room and play video games or browse the net on his computer (he had a better computer than me). So, while I am friendly, even outgoing at times, I will admit to making less effort as I get older to meet new people, the exception being neighbors as I have always felt that to be important. Neighbors are another interesting relationship; I am lucky that I have excellent neighbors all around me. You want to be friendly with a neighbour, have a good relationship, but you still want to give them privacy and not be a pest. Should you have all your neighbors over for dinner or a party? We have not done it and I am not sure. When we moved in a few years ago I was concerned over what the neighbors would be like, my fears were soon gone though as I met most of them and discovered I live on a quiet street (usually) with great neighbors who are happy to help you when you need it. I will say, however, that I have kept in touch with two neighbors from an old street we lived on, and I always like to catch up with them.

To get back to what I was saying at the beginning, for me the best (and most important) relationship I will ever have is with my wife, Joanne. I know it sounds corny, but it really is true, she completes my life and makes me a better person. When we met, I was twenty-three and almost finished my degree at university. I had tried many dating websites, been to bars, online chat programs, ads in the newspaper, clubs, friends, you name it, and none worked out. Suffice it to say while I had not given up on love, I was certainly discouraged and felt at times there was no one for me and I would spend my life alone. I was, quite thankfully, wrong and no matter what I do with my life I can say starting (and continuing) to love and work on my relationship with my wife is the best thing I will ever do. I truly believe that happiness is a cycle and for me I could not love myself (or anyone else completely) until I met her. This pandemic year was just another reminder about what a terrible mess I would be in if I had still been single. She means the world to me, and I love her with all my heart. I can be a hard person to live with on occasion, I have some annoying habits, I can be obsessive, argumentative, and maybe even a little bossy. I want to thank her here, publicly, from the bottom of my heart for all the wonderful years we have had together (over 20 total and over 16 years married). I love our life together and I cannot wait to see what the future brings, especially as we finish working and enter our retirement years.

People are social creatures, we need interaction, we need affection, and (virtually all of us) need to be touched, loved and made to feel special. I love to talk, and I need someone who I can talk to about random things like TV, comics, books, and role-playing. I am lucky in that since I was eighteen, I have had that friend; his name is John. I have called John about once a week for over twenty years now and we have had some great chats. We have often done things together just the two of us and he is always someone I can count on to get my drunk ass home from a party. While we usually agree on most topics, we have had occasional arguments and I value his honesty. I do not like to use the term best friend; I think every friend I have is different and are a different part of my life. But John is the friend I talk to the most and certainly this year during the pandemic, I have talked with him more than usual. I am thankful for his friendship, and I look forward to talking with him for many years to come.

I have gotten to know some other people quite well due to my writing. I have friends who are all in this writing group where we promote each other's books. They are people I have never met in person but with Zoom, e-mails, and Facebook I have gotten to know them, and they are all great people I am happy to have relationships with. I would also like to mention my editor, Heather. I have had four different editors (maybe five, I'm not even sure) but she is the one I have built a relationship with. We knew each other first from conventions (as authors who sold books and had tables) but with her editing a third book from me (this book of course), I feel she has gotten to know me as a person, and I value both our professional and personal relationship.

Again, not ranking but if I had to choose the other most important relationships it would be with my mom, brother, sister-in-law, and my niece and nephew. My mom (now more than ever since my dad passed a few years ago) is always there to love and support me, as is my brother. She has always given me good advice and is always there if I need someone to talk to, have a good meal with, or even just to listen while I spout off some wacky idea I came up with. I am fortunate that I am literally right now looking at my mom's and brother's houses right outside my window. We did not plan it that way but when we looked for a place to build a house a few years ago this was the only place that met all the requirements. The fact that I could walk to both houses in less than five minutes was just a bonus.

So, this is me saying that I am thankful for everyone I have had (or still have) a relationship with. I am lucky to have plenty of great friends that I have known for a long time and can fondly remember all the good times we have had.

Relationships are important, I would say even essential to being human. You must love yourself and then find the right people to love (though perhaps not always in that order). I do not think anyone needs a lot of friends and you must realize that eventually most (if not all) of your family will either die or move away. That is sad, but it is also the truth. Get the social connections you need, have a chat with your friend, spouse, or a family member. Find the loving relationship that completes you, whether it is with a partner, a pet, or even with yourself. Sometimes we all need help, we all need someone to cry with or just have someone who listens. If you do not have that person in your life, be that for someone else. Like anything in life relationships take work but also like many things, you get back what you put in and they are worth the effort.

Chapter 13: I'm Proud to be a Newfoundlander

This chapter is a little different than the rest. For this one I will be unabashedly talking about my love for the place I live, Newfoundland. But I will also talk about how it has drawbacks and how my plan is to one day leave the town I am living in and quite possibly the province as well. In case you are not great with geography (and I do not claim to be, so I can relate) Newfoundland and Labrador, Canada is the most easterly province in Canada. Half of our province is an island and we do not have a large population (about 520,000 when I last checked), yet we are geographically the size of some small countries (Cuba being a great example, at less than a third our size they have over eleven million people). In terms of population, that means Cuba has about twenty-one times the population we do! Labrador is the other half of the province as part of the mainland (which borders Quebec) but as I have never been there, I will be talking about the island portion of our province only. This is not a geography lesson, though, suffice it to say we have a lot of woods, lakes, ponds, beaches, and other areas where there are little to no people around. For the most part, however, I will be talking about my feelings and experiences with Newfoundland and of course some of the people I have encountered while I have lived here over forty years.

When you are young you do not have a strong sense of place. I just did not realize how special Newfoundland was until I was older. It was certainly my late twenties before the appreciation I have for my home really started to become a reality. I suspect many people say that when they grow up in a place with a smaller population that you have that hometown feel, you trust your neighbors and you do stuff you may not do in a larger city. When I was young, I did not have a cell phone. My parents asked where I was and I told them (usually) and I was back before dark, unless it was Halloween or some other unusual night. I walked home from school (which took about twenty to twenty-five minutes) from the time I was twelve years old (only on nice days of course), and nothing ever happened to me, and I never felt unsafe. On Halloween, my brother and I would head out, fill up pillowcases of candy and come back to dump them out, only to head out again. There was a neighbor down the street who made candy apples (oh how I miss having strong teeth) We went down and got them every year she made them. No checking candy, no worries about a homemade candy apple, I would eat it on the way back to the house. I know that you hear that all the time, but it was true, I do not know if the world was any safer or if people were less paranoid, but I almost never felt unsafe any time in Newfoundland.

To give a recent example of how Newfoundland is unique (and safe), we came home from work a few weeks ago (this was in November but there was no snow on the ground) and saw a note stuck in our door. Curious, my wife took it out and read it. It was from a total stranger who said they loved our house and wanted to buy it! The amazing part is that it had his name, phone number, and e-mail address. Where else in the world would someone not only go up on someone's house to leave a note but also give their contact info to a total stranger? I am sure there are a few places, but Newfoundland is certainly one of a select few in the world like that. We were flattered and while we are not moving (at least not for several years) my wife did text him to thank him for the offer. As another example, when I was a new driver, I went a little too fast and was not always mindful of the road conditions. I went off the road one winter night and was stuck in the snow. I made a futile attempt to get my car back on the road but soon gave up and got back in the car. Just as I was starting to dial on my cell phone (this was a big one that had to be plugged into the cigarette lighter—yeah, I am that old) and a person stopped to help. Soon after, another stopped and then a cab also pulled up and asked if we needed help. With four people we managed to get the Jeep back on the road and I was reminded of how friendly and helpful people in Newfoundland could be. It is worth relating another story on how Newfoundland is usually a safe place. My friend Heather was at a show in Corner Brook and noticed an empty car running in the parking lot when she went in. After two hours, she came out and found the car still there when a group of women (who had also gone to the show) got into it and left. Think about it, a car was running in a city for over two hours, and no one took it! I think it is fair to say that this is certainly an example of what small cities are like here in Newfoundland.

One final example, about ten years ago I was at a party at a fishing stage in the Battery (in St. John's). This road is at the bottom of a popular trail and so a lot of tourists (and residents) walk by the fishing stages. On this day a couple happened to poke their head in (the door was left open), and instantly a woman walked up to them and asked if they wanted to come in for something to eat. I could see the look of surprise on their faces, but the man agreed, and they came in. It was such a beautiful moment to see them sit down and eat with everyone else. They thanked the host profusely and said it was the friendliest thing they had ever experienced. They had German accents and confirmed that they were visiting Newfoundland from Germany (this was summertime) and I thought about it while I ate beside them. It is wonderful that we have kept our hospitality and that total strangers were invited into a party to eat and talk with other people. I know something like that does not happen every day in Newfoundland, but I know that it does happen, and it shows how friendly and inviting the people here can be.

Newfoundland is not just about the people; however, it is a special place as well. I had a fan of my books come to Newfoundland once and he told me that when he read my books, he felt that the place itself is like a character, it's so important to the story. So that got me thinking about how Newfoundland is a unique place. There is an island off Newfoundland (technically two) called St. Pierre and Miquelon, which is owned by France. We are the only place in North America where you can get on a boat and an hour later be in a place that is controlled and run by a European country. The French culture there is just like you would imagine, people greet each other by kissing on both cheeks, they have a more laid-back lifestyle with almost everyone taking a two-hour lunch break Monday to Friday. St. Pierre has traditional French cuisine (and more tourist-pleasing fares as well) along with amazing pastries, and of course, a different language. So, in about five hours I can leave my house, get a ferry and be in a part of France (sort of), and be back home the next day. I have been to St. Pierre many times and it is certainly a unique activity that I am lucky that I can do it.

In terms of what is right next to me, I can leave my house, walk or ride my bike, and within ten minutes be at the water or alone in the woods. I have seen animals roaming free (rabbits, cats, chickens, goats, even a bald eagle once). I've watched windsurfers give an impressive display in the ocean and boats of all kinds, and of course plenty of people, their dogs, kids, and once two people with their pet sheep out for a walk! One day I even met a woman on a horse, and have seen the occasional dirt bike, quad, and three-wheeler (yeah, we still have people who ride them here).

I cannot talk about Newfoundland without mentioning the weather. I realize that for a lot of people the weather is barely a consideration, its cold in the winter, hot in the summer, seasons change like they always do. Here it is a little different. While we are not known for getting hurricanes (though Hurricane Igor did a lot of damage in 2010) we are known for a lot of terrible and unpredictable weather. I know scientifically it must be because we are out in the middle of the ocean and near a cold ocean current but that does not make it any more normal. We get a tremendous amount of fog and being on an island you can literally watch it roll in sometimes from the ocean. Just earlier this month (I wrote this in November) we left work in crummy, snowy weather. Within ten minutes the snow got lighter and as we continued to go downhill and got closer to the water, there was no snow at all! This happens a lot here, but it continues to impress me how driving such a short distance you can get completely different weather. Literally my sister-in-law had her snowblower out this November night (she is about twelve minutes from our house) and we had no snow at all.

We are also known for the weather changing quickly. I remember one summer day I was out for a walk and within an hour the temperature dropped ten degrees, I had to go back to the car and get a sweater and this was in May! I marked on a calendar one year going a full two months without seeing the sun and an incredible amount of rain in that period. I hate bad weather, cold, wind, snow, fog, ice pellets, even rain. Suffice it to say I am someone who grumbles about the weather here a lot. While that sounds like a drawback (and to be honest it is), in a strange way it makes you really appreciate the nice days and get out and enjoy them.

This year while there was not a hurricane, we did have a terrible winter storm in January. You will have to forgive me, but this is such a great example of the dual nature of Newfoundland. You can both love and hate it almost at the same time! So, when this storm happened, I was ripping mad. We had snow drifts of four and five feet high all around our house and our driveway was worst of all. I knew this would have a major impact on my life (and it did for over a week) and I was anticipating a day of sheer agony as I saw how much work it would be to clear our driveway (yes, I have a snowblower, but the snow was higher than that!). After we had started clearing snow for maybe twenty minutes, my neighbor to the left came over to help. Then a few minutes later both neighbors to the right, also came over to help. So, in short order there were three people shoveling and two snowplowing, all to clear one driveway, step, and two doors! It still took over an hour (almost two) but without the help of my excellent neighbors, it would have taken two or three times as long. Newfoundlanders come together when someone needs help, and they help each other when times get tough. It made that day a lot easier, and it helped me face the next seven days when many things were closed. When people were able to start moving around the twin cities (St. John's and Mount Pearl) it was a little more bearable.

I must add another thing of note about the weather. Here everything seems to hang on the wind. If the wind blows from the right direction, it will be a warm day, but if it comes from the wrong way, it feels like it will cut you in two! I go for a lot of bike rides, and it is unfortunate that there are many days when it so windy that I must turn around and head away from the water. The wind here does drive me crazy. It does mean that air pollution here is low but not non-existent of course. Something I learned just this year is that studded tires create air pollution because they break up the pavement and release road particles into the air (Furberg, 2018) and the majority of people on the island use them every year.

About five years ago I was on a trip with my wife and parents to British Columbia (BC). One of the first things my dad said when we got there was "There's no wind!" and he was right. Here in Newfoundland, we are so used to it being windy that it comes as a shock when it's not around. I did some research, and it turns out that we had a period of about ten years where we had less wind. That period, however, has ended and we are back to breaking records. Sure, we get more wind in the winter than the rest of the year, but it is still true that "Newfoundland and Labrador is still a very windy spot" and has more wind warnings issued than any other spot in Atlantic Canada (Bird, 2019). This means that when you go somewhere else you are sometimes taken by surprise with how it is not so windy. We have our own ode, and one of the lines mentions 'windswept land' and it is as true today as when it was written in 1902 (Heritage, 2021).

This brings me to one of the things I really do love about Newfoundland, our long history. While there is no proof, it is assumed that the Beothuk were our original inhabitants. It is also interesting to note that it is possible that the Beothuk and the Vikings may have met and due to their violent nature, the Beothuk would become wary of future settlers. To be honest, Newfoundland has so much history and culture I could never do it justice here, so I will have to leave it up to you to find out more on your own. We are also one of the only places in the world with proof of a Viking settlement dating back to 1000 AD (Jansen, 2004). In terms of Europeans coming over, we were originally settled by the Vikings, but they did not stay. Most people considered Newfoundland's "discovery" (as the Viking's did not have many accurate maps) to be by John Cabot in 1497. So that means European settlers (and of course their descendants) have been living in Newfoundland for over five-hundred years.

When you go to some places, you can really see the history. For seventeen years I lived in a house that was over one-hundred years old, though to be honest we did a lot of renovations, and it did not have a historic status. I really feel our history when I am in downtown St. John's. It is an amazing mixture of old and new buildings. You can easily find a building that has been there for over a hundred years that is right next to a parking garage only built ten or fifteen years ago. Downtown is where I used to spend a lot of time when I was in university, going to bars, or just going for walks in the summer. Recently, this past summer, they closed off a street to vehicles and called it the Pedestrian Mall. There were already stores there so they just let shops and restaurants build out into the street with patios. It was a great idea that worked well, so I went three times and even stayed at a hotel one night with my wife to get the full experience. I have always loved history and to be around historic buildings, statues, and anything else with a past, gives me comfort and helps me to connect to a place.

It's not all smiles and sunshine here of course. Just in the past eight years the government has ran up a massive debt on this mega project called Muskrat Falls. Basically, they hired a company who had no experience in doing a mega-project, they went billions of dollars over budget and the project ended up being delayed first by months, then years. I think it goes back to the government just being short sighted, naïve and just plain careless with our money and our future (Roberts, 2019). Twenty years ago, we should have been a pioneer investing in green technology, instead we invested heavily in oil. Consequently, when the demand (and price) of oil drops, our economy suffers, and people move away. All that said I will admit that we have so much invested in the oil (and now hydro-electric) industry we have no other reasonable choice than to move forward. We can only hope that another oil boom comes and that this time the government will be more careful with how money is spent. Many years ago, my wife and I seriously considered moving away when we were both looking for work. The job situation worked itself out and we stayed, my only real change was living in Grand Falls-Windsor (the central part of Newfoundland) for about a year. As I said earlier, we do plan to move once we are retired, either to Corner Brook (on the west coast of Newfoundland) or possibly to one of the maritime provinces, like Prince Edward Island (PEI).

You get used to the place you live in, and you often do not notice the differences unless you travel. Just recently we were in Nova Scotia (a province right next to us) and my wife wanted to find an apple flip (you may know them by the more common term, apple turnover). You would not think it would be hard. We went to several stores, supermarkets, and even a farmers' market. But we could not find one in Nova Scotia. Perhaps they are a Newfoundland specialty? Every week we go to our corner store (just two streets up from us) and buy either an apple flip, goulash (like Hamburger Helper), or cookies, all hand-made by the store owner. I have met her lots of times and it is to the point where she puts posts on her Facebook page just so we (and some other people) will see them! These are just fun posts announcing the goulash is ready to buy, but still it shows thought and it certainly gives you the nice hometown feels.

Here in Newfoundland many people are proud of where they live and call anyone not from here (who lives in Canada) a mainlander. I suppose it could be considered a negative term, but I think it mainly just shows how unique Newfoundland is and how it gets in your blood somehow. I can honestly say that when I am not here, I just do not get the same feeling, not even somewhere as close as Halifax, Nova Scotia (which for me has too many people). NL is the kind of place where you can get Seaweed Gin (and it's delicious) along with blueberry beer from a micro-brewery that is just down the road from me (so I can walk there easily). We are a place with a small population but a lot of talented people, not just bakers or brewers, but artists, performers, athletes and yes even a few writers. We try to support local businesses and showcase the talents of people who live here on an ongoing basis. As a writer I have been paid by the library for copies of my books (all five of them as of this writing). I really do not like crowds and as I talked about earlier, and we do not have a lot of people here. So, while it is possible to be in a crowded spot, it does not happen often. I have gone to movies (in non-pandemic times) with no one else in the theater. I have been out for a walk and not seen another person for an hour or more, and I can be home from work (barring an accident, construction, or bad weather) in less than fifteen minutes. It is one of the reasons I think about PEI as an alternative, they have even less people in their province than we do, and I am the kind of person who is happy with just some people around. I know it is not a unique feature to Newfoundland, but the general lack of crowds (and traffic) is something that has always appealed to a deep part of my nature.

You need to find things you love about where you live, find things you enjoy doing and that makes you happy. While perhaps some of you reading this may live in truly miserable places, I am sure the vast majority live in nice towns or cities that may have enjoyable things to do there that you do not even know about. It can be something small, like just a few weeks ago a friend told me about a local company, The Oat Company, that makes granola type bars. We ordered a bunch (which were pricy, supporting local always costs a bit more) and they are yummy. We will certainly be getting more. If you love a place in your town, go there. If you believe a particular store, restaurant, or craftsperson can provide you with a great product, pay a little more and support it whenever you can. Life is one big balancing act. I buy stuff from Amazon, Walmart, and most of the other large chains. But this year has shown me more how vulnerable local businesses here are in Newfoundland are and I have stepped up my efforts to support them.

    I will finish with a song. I am not much for traditional Newfoundland music; it is folky and a lot of it sounds the same to me (Ron Hynes being a notable exception) but there is a particular song that always makes me think of home. Only here could you have a band called Buddy Wasisname and the Other Fellers (their actual name) and one of their biggest hits is "Saltwater Joys." It is by far their best song and is serious (with almost everything else they have done a joke) and talks about the love for Newfoundland and what keeps people here. I hope reading this chapter may cause you to come to Newfoundland someday, or at least will make you discover something special about where you live and maybe even how you could make it a little better.

Chapter 14: The importance of Being Vegetarian.

For this chapter I will try to keep it a little lighter and mostly informative. I am talking about being vegetarian and if this chapter makes you think about how much meat you consume and convinces you to eat less (meatless Mondays is a thing) or even become a vegetarian, than that is all I could hope for. I decided to become a vegetarian when I was twenty-nine. Believe it or not, back then one of the main reasons I decided this was not for health reasons, I was just bothered by the thought of having animals die so I could eat them, and I also found that the smell of cooking meat bothered me (with some meats I still feel that way to this day). I am past my forty-fourth birthday as I write this, so it has been over fifteen years and I have never regretted my decision to become vegetarian for one second.

It was not easy adopting this lifestyle for the first few years. My family was resistant to the idea and thought I would give it up in a few months (I did not). My wife found it to be a nuisance as she would often have to cook two meals (she still does but I do eat more sandwiches and salads that I prepare). Family get-togethers were often a hassle with a lack of food choices for me and there were restaurants where literally the only thing I could eat on the menu was plain rice and bread. People ask me why I became a vegetarian, and I think the most honest answer is that I did it for several reasons. besides my reasons above, it is better for the environment, you have a lot less man-made crap in your diet, I have never liked eating big meals, and I guess to be honest I like being different from other people. I did not just throw out all the meat in the house, which would have been terrible because my wife was not a vegetarian when I made the switch. I ate up the last of the burgers I bought. I gave myself a few more weeks to be certain I wanted to change my diet for the rest of my life and then told everyone I was giving up eating any kind of animal. I should add that I did see a graphic video (I think it was a documentary), showing how animals are killed for the meat industry and that certainly helped make up my mind. I would argue, though, that convincing people to become vegetarian by grossing them out with graphic violence is not the best way to start. Please forgive the next bit, my wife says I get preachy when I explain why I am vegetarian (at least she did years ago). It is also true that I was that vegetarian who was a member of PETA (People for the Ethical Treatment of Animals) and was outspoken on occasion. While I think PETA does help animals, and for years I would do every online protect e-mail or website click they had. I also eventually saw that they were too extreme for my tastes and sometimes misguided. I will give them credit; they do not like to lose members. When I stopped paying my membership fee, I got a whole bunch of letters, one final one that looked like it was signed by the head of the organization asking why I had left and hoping I would come back.

When I was a vegetarian at first, I suppose I bragged a little bit. I just felt proud of myself because I was not only a more humane person, but I also knew I was doing the environment a favor (I will explain that more later). Perhaps I was even helping smaller food places by buying more local or unusual vegetarian items. I was happy that I was putting less harmful chemicals in my body that meat often contains. I felt confident I would live longer and maybe even be happier than a lot of meat eaters. I also found that within a month or so I had more energy than I did when I ate meat, and I could snack more as I almost never get that over-full feeling I would get from a big meal with meat. I remember meeting a former professor years later. She was friendly, and we chatted for a minute in the hallway. During that conversation, she told me I had a certain glow about me. I agreed and attributed it to my being a vegetarian. Years later it still brings a smile to my face. Here I am twenty years later thinking about it, so it meant a lot to me then and it still does now. Somehow it made all the years I had been a vegetarian mean something, even if in nothing else I was a better version of myself.

Becoming vegetarian was just a great example of how to awaken your mind to new possibilities and realities of life. I love to research topics and when I heard of how being vegetarian helped the environment, I spent hours looking at articles on it, watched documentaries, basically became obsessed, but in a positive way. It is not complicated; if you are a farmer with cows, those cows pollute the environment with methane gas when they flatulate. We have way too many cows on the planet and so all this methane gas hurts the ozone layer that protects our planet. Of course, there is also the huge expense to house, feed, and look after all the animals on a farm in comparison to the cost associated with buying and planting crops. Plants are just way simpler and would produce more money for farmers because they could have so many more plants to harvest in comparison to animals. I am not a farmer and I know being a little more realistic that livestock would not just be taken from farms overnight, it would take time, and many would keep some animals, at least for a time. I found a great article where farmers talk about the benefits of having less livestock and more plants (in particular hemp for CBD products) (Levitt, 2020). I researched all about the growth hormones and steroids that large-scale farmers often put in their animals. It may not be just evolution that has made us much taller than people seventy years ago, it is possibly these chemicals entering into the meat, being eaten (or drank in the case of milk) by children and making them bigger than a generation before them. Aside from all these ethical reasons there was also the fact that I never liked any kind of seafood or wild game. I have had a love of carrot juice since I first tasted it at a café in downtown St. John's. I liked going to places that were different from the norm like vegetarian restaurants, and I got better at cooking things on the barbeque as I had to watch veggie burgers carefully (they tended to cook a lot faster than their meat counterparts). Some brands I would personally recommend are *Dr. Praeger's* (excellent burger with a bad name), *Beyond Meat Burger* (tasty but expensive) and *Yves* (pricey but good).

    I suppose like most people who are vegetarian, I became aware in the back of my mind when I ate meat that animals died for it. For a long time though, you just think, 'Who cares if an animal died for my meal? I am more important than a cow,' or 'that is what nature intended,' or maybe you just eat and never think about how your food was made. But I would argue that you should. Just as you should look at the world a little deeper sometimes, things are often not what they seem and sadly for virtually any decision we make in a modern world, there is some small consequence somehow.

    I think ultimately, I realized that it is wrong to think you are in any way better than anyone else, its more that you should realize that really the only person you should be in competition with is yourself. For me I think the best all of us can ever do to make ourselves a little better most days. I think the best way to convince a person (even for a small amount of time) to stop eating meat is to try and reason with them. To explain it simply that when you eat plants it is a direct connection between you and the vitamins you need. When you eat a cow, you are getting the benefit of the microbiomes which is from bacteria in the cow's stomach. The thing is you do not need to eat cows to get this, they are found in foods like yogurt, pickles, some cheeses and sourdough bread. I will not try to explain what a microbiome is and why you should have healthy bacteria in your guts, someone much more informed on the subject like Dr. Sam Westreich can explain it much better than I can (Westreich, July, 2018).

If you think about it logically, let's say you ran a business that depended on more milk and more meat from their cows, you will do whatever you could legally do to make those cows as big and as productive as possible. They have bills to pay and in a real way how much they produce in terms of milk and beef may mean something important or even drastic to them financially. Of course, I know these are usually larger farms (and yes, I know many farmers are able to do everything ethically and humanely with their animals with no growth hormones, but almost none of them are well known) but still the point is that many farms are still using these things and do not have to. I know we are not all going to run off and make a hippie commune with animals running about. I live in the modern world too, but if many people became vegetarians, then it could make a real difference with the environment and our health.

To sum up my reasoning, I would say that realistically about fifty percent is for the ethical feeling and the other half for less man-made garbage in my body. I almost never bring the political aspects of vegetarianism up, but a notable exception is the seal hunt here in Newfoundland. For me I am not just a vegetarian but a believer in animal rights (the two are usually linked in my experience) and I feel the issue is worth bringing up. It has remained a controversial topic for so long that I have tried to refine my response on it. Generally, what I say is that I am against the seal hunt, I usually put my reasoning on that it is a declining industry that will only get smaller and then non-existent. The demand (especially during the pandemic) combined with thinning sea ice has decreased steadily over the past few years and really the Canadian government just needs to make the decision to end it (in a realistic way by giving say a few years notice to people who still work in the industry). I know for Indigenous Canadians (and other Indigenous people) that hunting is a way of life, part of their tradition and history. I also know that I can respect a culture, such as those of Indigenous people, and not agree with it. I found an article that really puts the whole thing in perspective (and is the definition of irony), I hope you'll read it (Roberts, 2020.) The article talks about how hunters are worried about seal pups because of the thinning sea ice (due to climate change of course). While I am happy to see hunters concerned about the effect of climate change and the fate of seal pups, why then can they not see what is so obvious? Any hunting of seals needs to come to an end, they are already facing trouble with thinning sea ice and people are not even able to hunt them because of lack of said ice. I think if you are already concerned about seals (and the environment) that it's only small step in terms of your mindset to give up hunting them and possibly even take steps to help the environment.

So, you could experience your own little awakening with this or something else; maybe it is religion, maybe books, music, or whatever you can immerse yourself in. I can hope that whatever you become (or are already passionate about) will make the world a little better for yourself, even if only in your mind and understanding of truth. Further I can hope even more that as you will spread the word of a helpful truth you are passionate about, and this will make your corner of the world a little better. Regardless of all that, I will just say I hope you would just once try a "Meatless Monday." There is no possible way it will hurt and what I can guarantee is that it will help.

Chapter 15: Losing a Parent

When you talk about death, grief, and loss there is no avoiding the negative emotions that must come up. It is my hope that by the end you will (as I did) come to see that while it is hard to lose a loved one, it makes you value life more when you see someone else's end. It brings your own mortality in sharp focus and hopefully it lets you ultimately reflect not only on the life of the person you lost, but ultimately on your own life and how it is just a book divided up in chapters. I would like to start this a different way than the rest of the other chapters. Two years after my dad passed, we had a celebration of life for him. Lots of people came and it was a lovely, heartfelt evening. People spoke (including me, I read his favorite poem) and one of those people present was my aunt (his sister) Charlotte. With her permission I will reprint her words here. She did an amazing job describing my dad and talking about his life, you can read it for yourself in Appendix A (towards the end of this book). I think that the speech my aunt wrote was important to include as it gives you context on what my dad was like and a lead in to how his final days were spent.

My dad (Greg—his first name was Charles but only my grandmother ever called him that) was really a character and I miss him to this day. There is a song by Tom Cochrane where he says you only remember the good times and forget about the bad. I think eventually that comes to be the case but the way my dad died will stick with me for a long time and unfortunately it was not pleasant. I am just going to get this part over with and hopefully this chapter will brighten up in a few pages.

My dad was diagnosed with multiple myeloma back in 2014. The doctor at the time said that most people live five to seven years with it if they are lucky and the medications work well. She also said that usually it is not the myeloma that leads to death but complications that arise from it. Dad did not respond well to the medications, and he was not a good patient. He always wanted to be busy and had to do something, and I remember him falling off a chair while he was working on a light at home (this was after he was diagnosed). The doctor and the pharmacist warned him to be careful and slow down but that just was not him; he had to keep going as hard as he could. In lots of ways, I am glad he did. He still went on trips and enjoyed his life as best he could while dealing with all the medicines and hospital visits. Charlotte and I were often the ones who would take him to appointments. We would take notes as he usually did not care much about the details and then fill my mom in afterwards (she found the meetings stressful). I should have seen the warning signs, the medicines he took did not last as long as they should have, and he would be taken off one and put on another. My dad started to lose weight and had a lot of scabs on his arms due to the medications and the myeloma, but again this did not stop him. We were up on a roof in Florida just three months before his death, with blood running down his arm that he had cut and not even noticed. But that was him.

    I suppose I was in denial; I knew that he did not have a lot of time left but I still thought in April of 2017 (when he had to go in hospital as he was feeling so terrible) that he had at least a year or two left. But I would soon find out such was not the case. I will never forget the day the doctor came into his room. It was Mother's Day and when she first came in my aunt and uncle where there so she said she would come back later. As soon as we were alone dad said, "She doesn't have good news, you wouldn't leave when other people were here if it was good news." I do not remember my reply, I offered some platitude and waited for her to come back. I could see when she returned about fifteen minutes later that it was true. Her eyes were watery, and her face filled with sadness; it was almost like a movie when you knew the news was bad. She said that his myeloma had developed into plasma cell leukemia (another kind of blood cancer) and in her opinion he had about a month or less left. The crazy part was that it had been only a few years before when I was in a different hospital room with my dad (this is when he was first diagnosed with myeloma, that was a tough night) when a doctor came in and told another patient he had six weeks to live. I remember talking with my friends about it and saying silly things like "Can you imagine? What would you do if your life was reduced to six weeks? How would you cope?" and here I got to see what my dad would do. He cried of course, I was more in shock and tried to comfort him as best I could. I remember he tried to lighten the situation a little and said, "that doesn't even give me time to pick out a suit!" before the doctor left the room. Quickly though he composed himself and showed his true character. He knew mom was coming to see him soon that day and said, "You can't tell her right away, you have to give me time to break it to her slowly."

Of course, I had to agree, even though my emotions were already getting tied up in a knot and my head was spinning. I said I would keep this secret until he could break it to her. It turned out that he really could not keep it a secret for long as in the next week his decline truly began to rapidly occur. He was like me, always making plans, always dreaming of what he could do next. He had a small notepad near his bedside with phone numbers and ideas in it, he looked at me and said, "Well this is useless now.". He wanted to say it with anger, but he was just too devasted and it just came out sad and heartbreaking. For a long time after that it made me think similar thoughts; that one day everything I dream, and plan will be gone. I can only hope I can feel accomplished in my life when the end comes for me. I remember going home that day, it was sunny out, but the warm weather meant nothing to me, I was lost in a fog of hurt and confusion. It was one of those days where I was so grateful to be married. My wife was excellent through this day and many other tough days, I knew it would have been ten times worse if I had had to go through it alone.

After he was given a short amount of time to live, we all started to feel the exhaustion, and one family member was always there with him every day. We hired a retired nurse to sit with him several times a week. She was excellent, and it was certainly some help. This is not to say we gave up. We discussed what his options were with the cancer doctor. I went so far as to get a rushed passport for him in case we decided to bring him to the USA. I spoke with a cancer doctor in Boston and even arranged a phone call between him and his local doctor in Newfoundland. It was decided that he would get the same drugs/treatment in the USA as he was getting here, and it would only be under a different setting. We gave him a last chance with a large dose of steroids and while his numbers (I do not recall exactly what they were, they were blood/health related) went up, it was not enough to make a difference. Ultimately a nice woman came in to talk with us about hospice care. There is a place in St. John's which is mainly for people who are dying, and the idea is to give them some comfort and privacy in their final days.

When he went there in early June, I knew it was getting close to the end. As I said to a friend of mine a few months later, watching someone you love die and knowing there is nothing you can do (aside from making the person comfortable and showing love) is truly the most horrible feeling I ever had, and that notion barely left my mind for almost three weeks. I know that all our family suffered during this time, and I am not trying to diminish what they felt or went through. But I was there for a lot of his really bad times, and I felt as if every bit of joy and happiness I had in me were gone, and that my heart was broken daily.

Going back a little I want to talk about the good side of things. I do believe that no matter how bad a situation is, there is always a silver lining. I spent a lot of time with my dad (as did all the family and friends who came to see him) and in a sense I got to know him all over again. I even found out a few new things about him (or at least things I had forgotten). He talked about poetry and mentioned "If" by Rudyard Kipling and one called "The Shark" by Edwin John Pratt (a Newfoundland poet) about a blue shark. I remembered that it was because of my dad that I have such a deep love of classic rock. Songs like "Lyin' Eyes" by The Eagles were played to me by my dad when I was a baby and I love that song to this day. There was one night I will never forget that he woke up sometime around two in the morning. I had been asleep fitfully in a sort of cot near the foot of his bed. He told me a lot of his life story, leading up to how he met mom, got married, and how my brother and I were born. One of my only big regrets in life is that I wish I had encouraged him to talk. I could have handled another sleepless night; I wish I had recorded the whole thing so I could have listened to it afterwards. I suppose more than anything I wish there were more moments like that but as his body declined his mind did too and he spoke less and less. Eventually he was asleep all the time and unable to wake up.

A few years later we went to a movie called *A Beautiful Day in the Neighborhood* starring Tom Hanks as Fred Rogers. It was a wonderful movie that I highly recommend if you can handle some sad moments. While the movie has a lot of Fred Rogers (known by a generation as Mr.

Rogers) it is primarily about the relationship between a father and son who are estranged. The son is told that the father is dying and realizing that this is the last time he will have with him; he and his wife move in with the father to care for him in his final days. At a point in the movie the father (played superbly by Chris Cooper) wakes up in the middle of the night and wants to talk with his son. Suffice it to say it was so like what I experienced with my dad that it was a moving experience for me in the theatre. I have not re-watched the scene, but I encourage you to have a look, it will give you a really good idea about what I just described happening with my dad.

Aside from possibly saying more to my dad (and missing the exact moment he died, I was unfortunately in the other room), I did my best to care for him and help him to beat cancer. But like millions of other people, he lost that fight. I have no regrets about anything that happened before, he made the decisions about his treatment and drugs, and he was always stubborn and did what he wanted to do his whole life.

To give you an understanding of what he was like in terms of safety (or lack thereof) when I was about fourteen, he had a bad accident. He was using a chainsaw to cut above his head through a wall (that he had not checked for nails). These are two things you are never supposed to do. He struck a nail, and the chainsaw came back and struck him in the face! Suffice it to say he was extremely lucky, it hit the bone just below his eye, but he did not lose the eye and was sent home that night. The doctor said if he had struck even a centimeter higher, he would have likely bled to death. Instead, Dad joked about the stitches he got and was back at it the next day. I am convinced that what happened to my dad was that he slowly poisoned himself with harmful chemicals like copper arsenate and chromium. He spent months cutting up pressure treated wood indoors, this is something you are supposed to do with a mask outside, but he would not have listened. He told me just before he died, "I've been lucky my whole life and my luck ran out."

When he first died, I will be honest, I was relieved. Not because he was gone but because his suffering was over and while there were brief moments of levity and laughter over his last few weeks, they had dwindled to none toward the end. I am not going to discuss each of the well-known stages of grief both because it is not needed and because I do not think I even went through them all. I was just sad, probably mildly depressed for a long time, maybe a year or more. That did not stop me from doing things with my life. While my dad was dying, I was doing the final edits on my short story collection, and I made myself finish. I put a dedication to him at the front of the book and even had a book launch later that year. I think the most obvious symptom for me with grief was sleep. For months I almost never had a good night's sleep. Even now in 2020, I still sometimes have dreams about him. While they are usually pleasant, he offers some advice or says everything is fine, sometimes they are not. I will see him younger and healthy only to realize in the dream that I know he is gone and be unable to wake from it right away.

For the first year or two after he passed, I would wake up early from dreams about him and have a really hard time getting back to sleep. I did not have a lot of time to wallow in grief, we moved twice by the end of 2017 (the year he died) and went on with vacations, holidays, birthdays, work and everything else in my life. My dad was a pack rat, which is just another way of saying he was a hoarder, and we were left with a tremendous amount of stuff to get rid of. I did what I could but even after three years some of the heaviest stuff remains in the woods, now hidden by grasses and bushes for most of the year. More sentimental objects like his antique motorcycle (a Triumph) are still around as no one has the heart to sell it. I realized by the summer of 2018 that I just had a miserable past year, and I just could not get back to writing. My dad always encouraged me to write and was there for all my book launches when he was alive (including giving a great speech at the first one which I wish had been recorded) and I did return to writing novels, putting out my fourth (and most likely final) vampire book in 2019.

I next tried to do an interview book on my dad. I discovered it was just too time consuming and difficult to interview all his friends and relatives, but I knew that I would write about his death when I was ready. That same year in 2019, we had a celebration of life for my dad. It was a wonderful, cathartic experience that did help me say goodbye to him in a shared way. I think what you learn (to paraphrase something my wife said about the death of her mom) is that you will always have a piece of grief wedged in your heart, you just come to accept it and learn how to be happy again. Another friend of mine said that when you lose a parent in the physical world they are not truly gone; you still have dreams about them and even carry out full conversations. In my experience it is true but often I just think about my dad when I hear a certain song he liked (and I did too), or when I look at the ocean, a boat, or even do something funny and have a laugh. My dad had a great sense of humor and had us in stiches many times.

My dad left me with some great advice. He told me about how he always viewed life as an adventure and maybe death was the grandest adventure of all. He talked about how he hoped he would see one of his best friends again without ever mentioning heaven. He talked about business (my mom and dad started our family beauty business) and the importance of never screwing anyone over in a business dealing. While I am against any kind of organized religion, I do not rule out the possibility of perhaps being in contact with people we cared for after death. I have also always felt that life is kind of like a game or adventure. For a long time, I engrossed myself in fantasy and make believe, my adventures were often imaginary, and I often had times where this pretend world was more enjoyable than my real one. Now I see that while my hobbies are important, the most rewarding thing you can do is explore the world (even if it is just near where you live as I was forced to do more in 2020 than ever before) with someone you love. I will never have the love of boats he did, I never see myself buying one, but I do love to look at the ocean and I am not averse to being on a boat occasionally. I see that spending time on a boat is a way to be at peace with yourself and the world around you, for me that is more akin to riding a bike, swimming, or just being still and trying to find the beauty in a moment when I am by myself. I will never be the businessperson my dad was, I think I have made good choices with my money most of the time, but I do believe that any important deal is worth being honest with the other person.

Ultimately, I realized the ways in which I am like my dad and what he gave me. He told me about how he watched *Star Trek* when it first came on the 60s, and I have been a *Star Trek* fan since I was four (no doubt partly due to him). I have a tattoo of the *Star Trek* communicator, was president of a *Star Trek* fan club in university and continue to watch the shows and movies today. My old-fashioned taste in music (I like little past the year 2000 and mostly love '70s and '80s music) and the fascination with really listening to lyrics and trying to figure out what it says about my life came from him. He influenced my love of seeing concerts and listening to music to help me relax. He loved television shows about history, and I also have love of history and can watch almost any documentary or well-done non-fiction show. He loved movies and while he did not go to many, I have always been a huge fan of going to theaters and of course watching them at home. For many, many nights (and mornings on the weekends) I would get great pleasure picking out movies I wanted to see. Without a doubt my love of travel was instilled by my dad, and I am forever grateful for all the fascinating and fun places he took my mom, my brother, and I to. He taught me how to not be afraid of people from other cultures and other places, as he had an ability to talk to someone wherever he went and could be rather outgoing and even a little charming when he wanted to be.

He loved to barbeque and that has become the only kind of cooking I enjoy. He was a fearless person in going to places and doing things that most people would not, and while I will never be quite that brave, I do have a love of exploring and will continue to go visit different places in the world for as long as I can. I was immensely proud of the fact that he was something of a rebel and would break lots of small rules whenever he could (I do the same when I do not see any harm in it). He had this natural talent to make you laugh and loved to see people happy, I sometimes find myself doing the same, trying hard to be positive, funny, and generally give people something to smile about when I can. He had some sobering thoughts as well; he told me how holidays were not a big deal, not birthdays, Father's Day, not even Christmas. They all become just another day eventually and he was right. While it might sound grinchy I find now in my forties that Christmas does not hold any meaning for me anymore. A couple of family gatherings are nice but mostly it is the same thing every year, with the main difference being you just have less people show up and more relatives die as times goes by.

I suppose that one of the hardest things about having a parent die is that you look up them so much and for so long, you see that as an example of strength and a constant in an everchanging world. When my dad was dying, this display of strength became a physical shell (for only the last part of his life, granted) but someone I thought would be around for a long time to come was no longer a part of my life. Everyone must face the death of a parent at some point in their life, and the unlucky few face both parents being taken at the same time. I think ultimately what I take away is another thing he also used to say that is true, the older you get, the quicker time goes by. I think about that a lot, just how much time had passed in my life and how my twenties now seem so far away, my teenage years almost feel like a movie, and I see myself as such a different person. I think about the time I have wasted, about things I pursued and focused on that never really made me happy. I can see now how much more important it is to just do a few things that you enjoy the most and even then, not to excess, everything in life needs a balance or as my dad would say "All things in moderation." I think I am more productive now and have cut out activities I do not enjoy so much. There are some people I see less often and that is a good thing for me.

    I could go on for quite some time as I lay in bed thinking on this Friday in December, but I think I will leave you with one other thing my dad used to say. He talked about how you did a job not because you liked it but because one day it would give you the freedom to do all the things you really wanted to do. Something I have had to accept is that I will never be defined by my job, I never would call it a career as some people might; it was just one of the larger periods in my life. I hope that I am only halfway through my own journey on this blue rock spinning through space. I hope that the best years for me are yet to come. I will try to do what any son can do, pick up the best pieces of my dad, make them my own, and try to do things a little better than he did. It almost comes down to a parent's path is a way that you can see how a life could be done, a good blueprint, but what you do with the design and exactly how unique you make it, that is a challenge we can all strive towards for this day and all those that come after

Chapter 16: The Geeks Will Inherit the Earth

I never really spoke enough about one of the things that most defines me as a person—my geekiness. So, let us get this clear, a geek is interested in something like science-fiction, fantasy, horror, or comic books. This person may or may not be socially awkward (I'd argue that is becoming less the case as time goes by). Whereas a nerd was originally just someone who does well in school or academic subjects and is also socially inept, usually not athletic, and often picked on in school for not fitting in with the cool kids. For me I was half and half (though I would call myself a geek now) as I did do well in school, but I have always loved sci-fi, fantasy, horror, comic books, basically hobbies that were not mainstream at the time. I hope that things are different in schools now but when I was there, I was made fun of because I loved comics, Dungeons and Dragons (D&D), *Star Trek*, *Star Wars* and other related things.

This chapter is both a celebration of how far geek culture has come and how everyone should be able to find a hobby or interest that they love and that brings them joy. I had accepted for a long time that my interests would be something that only a small group of friends and I would enjoy. Sure, there were conventions, movies, and clubs but I never thought any of it would be popular or well-known. Such was the case for a long time until about 2001. That was the year *The Lord of the Rings: The Fellowship of the Ring* movie was released. For those who don't know, J.R.R. Tolkien wrote three main Lord of the Rings novels (along with prelude and some other materials) way back in the 1930's with The Hobbit released in 1937 and the main three coming out in the 1950s. While these books are loved by his fans, they were never mainstream (though they did sell over 150 million copies) and only crappy animated film versions of it were originally made and I thought that is how it would stay (Wikipedia, 2021). When it was announced that Peter Jackson was going to direct all of the Lord of the Rings movies (only three were planned at that time) I was cautiously excited. At the time Jackson was not a household name and I really did not know how he would handle them. Once the movie was released, I was rather pleasantly surprised. *The Lord of the Rings* was wonderful and had (almost) everything I could have hoped for in an adaptation of a classic fantasy novel. It won Oscars (4 of them in fact) and made a ton of money. Little did I know, the truly amazing part was still to come.

Fast forward a few years and the final *Lord of the Rings* movie called *The Return of the King* did fantastic at the box office. It is an amazing movie (that is just a little too long) and won 11 Oscars! This was the first fantasy movie ever to win Best Picture and Best Director and tied with *Titanic* and *Ben-Hur* as winning the most Oscars of any movie ever. Suffice it to say I was rather pleasantly surprised and soon after that entertainment (and society itself) began to change. Geek movies were serious money makers and award winners for the first time ever and comic book, sci-fi and fantasy movies and TV shows started to come out in force. My favorite comic book character is Batman and when Christopher Nolan was slated to do three films about him, I was quite excited. This time all the movies made money (the second one simply called *The Dark Knight* made over a billion dollars, at the time only the fourth movie to ever do so) and even Oscars were within their grasp. Heath Ledger died just after he finished filming his role as the Joker and when he was nominated for an Oscar, I really hoped he would win it and he did! For the first time ever someone playing a comic book character won an Oscar (for best supporting actor). Suffice it to say geeky movies were here to stay with awards, money, and lots of media attention when they were good and deserved it.

Worth noting is sometime later (2019) Joaquin Phoenix also won an Oscar for playing the Joker, this time he got Best Actor. I know that it was the performances of Ledger and Phoenix that earned them Oscars, but it cannot be ignored that the Joker is an excellent character worthy of exploration in movies (and television). It is a fact I love to talk about, a comic book character effectively getting two Oscars is incredible! Of course, one other mention I must make is *Avengers: Infinity War*. This film came out in 2018 and it has the distinction of being the first comic book themed movie to ever earn two billion dollars at the box office. Two billion! I do not think if I you told anyone twenty or more years ago that a comic book would do that, they would believe you, I certainly never thought it when I was alone outside reading a comic down by the ocean that such a thing was possible.

I am not forgetting about *Star Wars*. Not only did the prequels (the crappy ones with Jar-Jar Binks) make a huge amount of money but they also showed how amazing special effects could be and what the film industry could do with the right technology. When Disney bought Marvel Studios this included the comics and TV shows, and the ability to make movies and almost all the Marvel comic book characters (it was a very profitable choice by them). We saw how a connected movie and TV universe could work. Disney began a new era of a quick succession of comic book movies and shows (both *Star Wars* and Marvel), all connected and building large storylines (which millions of serious fans like me adore). Just recently a show on Disney+ called *Wanda Vision* was nominated for 23 Emmys, including several for acting, one for writing and one for a limited series. Even more impressive is comic book adaptation shows, "aren't just an exceptional part of the Emmy nominations – they're leading the charge." (Vary, 2021).

More recently a show called *Game of Thrones* came out and it took the world by storm. It made all kinds of money, won awards, and was the most watched show on a paid channel (this was just before HBO had their streaming service for most of the eight seasons it was on). I would be at work and there would be a meeting that partially involved an actress from *Game of Thrones*. No, I do not do anything interesting like work in the entertainment industry, I work in the beauty industry (yeah not what you were expecting if you know me, maybe someday I will get into that in another book). Sophie Turner was a Wella spokesperson (company that makes hair products), so when she was signed on with the company it was a big deal. Once the show had been on a few years, however, I really started to see how *Game of Thrones* show had started to change the world a little. A staff member and I (along with my sister-in-law who also works there) would get in heated discussions on *Game of Thrones* and endlessly discuss how we felt the show would end. I often do deliveries for work, and I found myself in hair salons having long, detailed discussions about *Game of Thrones* episodes, books, and even the comics on occasion. I have been involved with the hair industry really my whole life and again never had I ever imagined that I could talk with five or six hair stylists about a fantasy TV show that has magic, dragons, other strange creatures, and even zombies in it.

   I love having women to talk with about geeky topics, and for most of my life it was such a rare thing that I never thought it would happen at work. When I realized that *Game of Thrones* was such a worldwide phenomenon, I had thoughts about how cool it would be to meet the writer of the books, George R.R. Martin, or go to some of the places it was filmed. I got a chance to do both of those things in 2019 when my wife and I (along with three other couples) all went to Ireland for a holiday. We got to meet George R.R. Martin at a convention that was happening in Dublin, Ireland. We also took a bus tour that brought us to places where the *Game of Thrones* show was filmed (this was in Belfast, Northern Ireland which is still part of the United Kingdom) and I loved the tour. Ireland has a rugged, rocky coast much like Newfoundland does, so if you want to go somewhere other than a hot, sandy beach, I recommend Ireland. *Game of Thrones* is a show I dearly love (and yes, I know the quality went down a lot by season 7 and really plummeted in 8) but it gave me some great moments, something to look forward to every week.

   Another great example of a show that really changed how people feel about geeks would be *The Big Bang Theory*, which was for several years the highest rated show on network TV (and lasted an incredible twelve seasons). For a while you could literally start up any conversation with anyone under the age of maybe fifty-five just by mentioning it. It has been syndicated on so many networks (even before the show ended, they were showing re-runs on other channels all the time) that it also became (albeit briefly) a worldwide sensation. Think about the number of times you used to see a "Bazinga!" shirt when the show was popular. I think it showed just how much society had changed. The main characters of the show (excluding Penny) were all huge geeks or nerds, one of them was so socially awkward at first, he could not even speak to a woman! While I have issues with the show (I gave up long before it ended, the quality went way downhill) I will never doubt the impact it had in terms of seeing geeky people in a different way. By showing their activities like video games, board games, D&D, going to movies to be fun, and things the characters really enjoyed, I think it made a lot of people consider that maybe some of these things really could be fun and just maybe their whole attitude towards geeks/nerds needed to change a little. They had incredible celebrity guest stars and I think they showed what a simple (yet enjoyable) activity it is just to go down to the local comic bookstore and chat with the owner. As someone who was literally starting to go to comic bookstores myself when I was thirteen to talk to the owners, it pulled hard on my geek heart strings for a while.

I have loved *Star Wars* for almost my whole life, and I will be the first to say it has had its ups and downs in terms of quality. *Star Trek* is (usually) more serious sci-fi steeped in science, with emotional storylines, character development, and is well-known for dealing with important current issues and pushing the boundaries of what is acceptable on TV (they even had to put a warning before an episode of *Star Trek: Deep Space Nine* for two women kissing, how times have changed). *Star Wars* when it is at its best does not need to do any of the things *Star Trek* does, it just needs to be bring me back to when I was a teenager and was excited to see what new thing *Star Wars* was doing. *Star Wars* awakens my inner child, and it sweeps me up in emotion and excitement. I get invested in the characters and while I know in the end the good guys will always win, it was still a lot of fun to watch Darth Vader cut through people like they were blades of grass. A little over a year ago *Star Wars* launched their first ever live-action TV show on Disney+ and I fell in love with *Star Wars* all over again with *The Mandalorian*. It just did all the things that I wanted it to do, characters behaved in a way I would have written if I was in charge and yet they still managed to come up with some great surprises and end season one on a high note. Then came season two, and I will say right away it was off to a slow start. For the first time ever, I could watch a *Star Trek* show and a *Star Wars* show every week and for the first two weeks *Star Trek: Discovery* was much better. Then with the third episode of The *Mandalorian* this season they just hit the gas and it was non-stop excitement and fun. As a *Star Wars* fan, it was a moment I had waited for my whole life, young Luke (as compared to old Luke from later movies) who was powerful with the force and kicking serious butt! Seeing Luke tear apart these Dark Troopers (who were powerful droids) brought me more moments of happiness than almost anything else that whole year. 2020 was a rough year and *The*

Mandalorian brightened up an hour of my life each week. It was like for that time each week I got to be a twelve-year-old again and I loved it.

It ties in well to an article I just read called "Rise of the new geeks: how the outsiders won" (Harrison, 2013). The article does a deep analysis of what I spoke about earlier, how society is changing, and how geek culture is more now a part of the mainstream. It also brings up the important point I just mentioned. People need to find an escape from their ordinary lives. If you love your job and find it a pleasure to go work then good for you, but the reality is that about sixty percent of people either dislike or hate their jobs, and I am one of them (Jones, 2020). The point is that I have always wanted an escape from real life. Unless you are blissfully unaware of the world, I do not think anyone is truly happy all the time. The world wears you down at times and shit happens. The important thing (for me and I am sure others) about being a geek is finding a way to escape your troubles and worries for a time. As usual, I do not mean you should spend so much time watching *Star Wars* that you neglect other aspects of your life. I mean that if you want to devote all your free time to collecting and painting miniatures (that is an *IT Crowd* reference) and it makes you happy, do it! As we live longer that means most of us will be working well into our 60s or even early 70s. You need something to take your mind off the rat race that is your Monday to Friday grind.

Once again, I will be honest, I could write and write about how much being a geek is a part of my life and what it has done to shape me, but I think that is enough. Maybe that escape for you is bowling, knitting, baking, or even watching trashy reality TV. Geeking-out on something is just embracing a part of yourself that makes you happy, finding an outlet for it and hopefully finding other people to talk about it with. For years now I have been calling my close friend John whenever I see a new episode of *Star Trek* (in its various iterations), *Game of Thrones* and now *The Mandalorian* I enjoy my chats with John on these shows a lot and if I am in a bad mood, I will call John, chat for a good 20 minutes or so and feel better afterwards.

In late 2020 a local comic bookstore owner died, and I realized I would never be able to go there and have a chat with him again. It is sad and I will miss him but what I must take away from it was how lucky I am to have other people to talk to. I know something I can do on a weekly basis (or sometimes daily if there is a great series, I want to binge watch) that will make me happy and life a little better. That is what being a geek means to me and I hope that you will find something that does the same for you and brings a smile, a laugh, or even a jolt of excitement into your life when you need it the most. I often go to a local marijuana store (legal in Canada since 2018) and I found myself one day talking with the clerk for a good fifteen minutes about *Batman* and comic books. It was a great surprise but showed what I have been talking about. The world is now full of people into geeky things, you just need to make the effort to find them and start up a conversation. I think one of the most important tips I can give is to stop wasting time on things that do not make you happy (whenever possible, I know you must pay bills), once you do that the better off you will be.

Epilogue: I've Learned a Few Things About Life

I am not bragging by any means about my knowledge or wisdom. Like most people, I made mistakes. I had failures, disappointments, and struggles. I hope with this book you do not take anything I say as gospel (see how religion sneaks in there? I am not even Catholic anymore and it just came naturally)! I hope you question everything you read here. Your experiences could be different than mine, they could be a lot better but in either case they are yours. I hope that this book may get a few people in a few important positions to make some changes in their lives and that could have a ripple effect. I want to make the world better when I leave, not worse. But I am sidetracked already. I think this was the other thing I learned, and I hope you will accept, is what writing (and life) are like; you think about things (not always in a sequential order) and your mind jumps around and that is what life does, it pulls you in different directions.

I am an obsessive planner; I just cannot help doing it with many aspects of my life. While I am happy when plans work out, you must accept that many times things just do not go as planned. It is the same in life. I had all sorts of ideas about what my life would be like at forty-four, but they are certainly not how it turned out. Now I will be clear, I am happy, and my life has turned out well, but I would be lying if I said I do not wonder how it might have been different. The road not taken is something most people wonder about from time to time. I have learned that you can have plans but then be prepared to scrap those plans and deal with what life gives you, because it will happen more and more often the longer you live. I did not think my dad would be gone when I was forty-one but that is what happened. The sentiment that 'life is short' always sounds cliché, but it is true. Do not waste moments and put off things you want to do, you never know when (or if) you will have the chance again. If you love someone tell them, spend time with them while you can and try to be understanding when they are in pain or do not act like themselves—you could be there one day.

While it might date this book, I also must put in that a few days ago Joe Biden and Kamala Harris won the US election (finally some good news this year). It also ties in with what I've learned that you can't just give up when things get tough. We aren't in end times, it's been a rough year, but things will get better just as they always do. As my mom is fond of saying; neither the good times, nor the bad times are lasting and that is an important lesson for us all.

I see that life is about making as many correct choices as possible but not sweating much over the bad ones. Life is about learning from your mistakes. If you can avoid making the same mistake twice, you have made your life a little better. Find pleasure in the simple things in life, while it would be great to say that every day is wonderful and amazing, stuff happens to us all the time, that's just life. Life is ordinary, banal, even boring most days but when you find a moment that you get to do something you love, savor it and find a way to repeat it. Of course, I do not mean get addicted to heroin or some other hard drug, I mean a healthy habit that brings you (and possibly even someone else) pleasure. This year like a lot of people I found the first few months of the pandemic hard, so much so that I went to my doctor and talked to him about it. He told me that you must find the time to focus on things that make you happy. I love to ride my bike and so I did that. I love a few TV shows and unless there is a reason I cannot, I watch them every week with the volume turned up. I love comics and I read them every week, generally four or more. I love animals and I spend time with our two cats as much as I can and try to go to places where I can see other animals. This summer I realized I was not getting anywhere outside the province with COVID and so we went around the province, returning to places we love like Trinity, Bonavista, and Green's Harbor. I think the best part of St. John's is the downtown area so when the city announced the Pedestrian Mall, I went there three times and enjoyed every visit.

We live in times where we are presented with so much misinformation, misdirection and plain lies on a continual basis that I would agree that sometimes it can be hard to distinguish what we have been told (or heard) and what the truth is. It can be a tough balance deciding when to speak your mind or keep your peace, knowing that governments lie but realizing that they are not lying when it comes to safety measures during a pandemic. The fact that anyone is capable of even making the argument that wearing a mask during a pandemic is a political statement, is so out of touch with reality it is hard to comprehend.

I firmly believe that you get back from life what you put into it. On days I get stuff done (which on the weekend can be as simple as a few hours of riding my bike) I feel better, there is more spring in my step and life seems a bit brighter. I also believe that you must have positive people in your life. You want people around you that make you feel better and see the positive in all things; the alternative just makes you feel worse. For someone who is obsessive, one of the hard truths I have had to accept is that the best moments in life often come with compromise and variety. If you do anything too much or dwell on it too often, you will only find disappointment and could end up pushing away the people who care about you.

I think one of the most important things I have learned is that no matter what, you need someone to share your life with. It sounds hokey as all hell, but it is true. What is the good of having amazing accomplishments if you have no one to share it with? We are social creatures and while it can be nice to spend a few days by yourself (or maybe even a week), a lack of human interaction just makes you feel lonely and isolated. If you do find someone who loves you and makes you happy, hold onto them with everything you have. Enjoy your time together and always try to see any problem from your partner's point of view.

I did not see it when I was young (and by young, I mean less than 32) but now I do; you go through clear chapters in your life. The early chapters are almost written by someone else because you do not have much control over your life. But once you get in your 20s things get interesting. I have had some amazing chapters, some sad ones, others that were just ordinary and of course the strange and funny ones we all experience. I am healthy and I exercise so I would like to think I am about halfway through chapter four of a nine-chapter book. So, while I spend time looking back, fondly remembering the past, laughing at the fun times and, yes, sometimes wishing things could be like they once were, I am mostly looking forward. I am excited about where my life will take me, and I dream about it all the time. I hope your life is like that and the best years are yet to be written. I dearly love music and I cannot end this book without a song recommendation. I have been listening to "Everybody's Free (to wear sunscreen) by Baz Luhrmann for twenty-three years now, it gives all the advice you will ever need in life. I hope you will give it a listen sometime and see what it can teach you.

Appendix A

Author's Note:

This speech was written by my aunt (and godmother) Charlotte Purcell for my dad's celebration of life. She does such a wonderful job of capturing stories from my dad's life and his character that I had to include it here. Ideally this should be read before reading Chapter 15.

"Greg O'Keefe was born on this day August 25, 1945. He was born to Cecily Langer O'Keefe and Charles O'Keefe and he had a big sister Roberta who was two years old when he was born. Seven years later I was born, Charlotte.

Mom and Dad owned and operated a grocery and confectionary at 69 Hamilton Ave. Bobby, Greg, and I grew up in the store, went there for our lunch from Mercy and St. Bon's. We worked evenings, weekends shift and summers covering off vacations for the staff. Bobby moved away to school when I was nine and shortly after that Greg and I started working Sunday mornings together, 9:00 to 1:00. We had fun and it was busy. That is where we began learning customer relations and believe me, we had some colorful customers go in and out of that store.

Greg was a St. Bon's/Brother Rice boy, but he hated school. He always said school got in the way of his learning. I remember Dad waiting impatiently out in the car for Greg in the mornings, beeping the horn, and Greg rushing through the door, hair stuck off, Mom chasing him trying to smooth it down and Greg saying, "Bruur don't care mom. Bruur don't care."

I remember Greg always wearing his white V-neck tee shirts. He loved them, but hated to take them off, so he would put his deodorant on under his arms on the tee shirt.

He loved his green Army jacket with the fur around the hood and wore it to skating at the stadium. Greg would ask Dad for $5.00 for skating, then he'd ask for money for the bus, Dad would say, "I just gave you $5.00." and Greg would say "but I don't want to break that" And that was Greg.

He cut Christmas trees and sold them out of our back garden on Leslie Street, and of course saved enough money to buy his motorcycle at age sixteen. He loved that bike, I would lie in bed and listen to him go up Leslie Street, Hamilton Ave, Bennett Ave. I could hear him to the lights at LeMarchant Road. He loved it. Greg had his bike refurbished and planned to ride it over to this 70th birthday party but his legs just weren't strong enough to hold it up.

Greg had a few jobs, on the boats, the *Glomer Serta* - or *Dirty Sertie a*s he called it but his first introduction to the beauty supplies business was with R.P. Godden. Old Mr. Godden was good to Greg and Greg liked him. First when Greg started Mr. Godden gave him cases of Women's Feminine hygiene products to go out to the stores and sell. Greg didn't skip a beat. He'd chat up the girls, they all loved him, then he'd leave the product on the counter with the information and ask them to have a look, he'd have to run out to the car for a bite of a sandwich or whatever, and when he'd go back in, they'd take whatever he had brought in. He sold the whole works of it that day.

Greg did so much in his life. He learned to fly a plane, took lessons in Newfoundland and Florida, He sailed boats back and forth from Florida to the Bahamas, The Great Lakes to St. John's, all around Newfoundland. He explored thirty islands in Placentia Bay, He built boats, marinas, houses, and he knew how to make money. He scuba dived for years, he loved that nobody could see what he was taking. But he was still the guy who pulled his car over to pick up a good piece of rope and made a trip to the bank to deposit $20.00.

At nineteen Greg met Regina Renouf, the love of his life, the perfect girl for Greg although I remember my father saying, "that ring will go across the floor more than once!" when they got engaged. Greg and Regina built their lives and business together. They worked as a team, they argued and fought but they always laughed and loved each other. No decision was made unless both agreed and discussions would go on into the wee hours of the morning, calling out from room to room, thinking. Talking. Even in their sleep they talked to each other, if you ever slept in the same house with them you'd know what I mean.

Greg loved his boys. Protected them, looked after them, trained them, supported their dreams and goals. He was so proud of Charlie, attaining his master's degree at MUN, writing and publishing his books and so proud of Andrew his baby and how he took to running O'Keefe Agencies like a fish to water. And today he's proud of how both his boys are caring for their mom.

When Sara Rose came along, she changed Greg, he became softer and teary eyed when he looked at her - his first grandchild. And beautiful Gregory, Greg did everything he could before he died to ensure Gregory would be cared for forever.

Pam and Joanne were the daughters he didn't have. They quickly became a big part of the O'Keefe family, working in the business. When Greg got sick, Pam and Joanne were there, among the few he allowed to care for his needs.

Greg was so funny, and bad funny as I'm sure you all know. Dropping his pants to the floor at O'Keefe Agencies - wonder he wasn't arrested, stealing anything that wasn't nailed down just for the fun of it. He and Daphne fighting over a piece of luggage that fell out of a car on a Florida highway. When the owner showed up for it, he had the guy show ID and tell him what was in the luggage to prove it was his.

Greg loved his friends and his friends loved him. There were no airs about Greg. He was who he was, kind, generous, smart, funny, dependable, a risk taker, knowledgeable, deep, soft.

Greg did not want to die. He hated being sick. He never accepted that he was sick or that he was dying so today I feel his spirit is here with us. His hat is there on his urn and if you look closely, you'll see Greg's face.

So, on behalf of Greg's family I want to thank everyone for coming here today and for keeping Greg's memory alive. He's here and he'll be here with us forever."

References

Chapter 1: My Thoughts on Writing

Tartakovsky, Margarita. "The Power of Writing: Three Types of Therapeutic Writing." *PsyhCentral*, Healthline Media, 19 January 2015, psychcentral.com/blog/the-power-of-writing-3-types-of-therapeutic-writing#1

Chapter 2: The Environment

Blog. "Lakes Not Waste Dumps Background to the Sandy Pond Alliance Court Challenge." *MiningWatch Canada*, 25 February 2013, miningwatch.ca/blog/2013/2/25/lakes-not-waste-dumps-background-sandy-pond-alliance-court-challenge

CBC. "Dumping mine waste in Sandy Pond senseless: NDP." *CBC-Radio Canada*, 24 July 2008, cbc.ca/news/canada/newfoundland-labrador/dumping-mine-waste-in-sandy-pond-senseless-ndp-1.726277

Eaton, Jeremy. "More junk than plant life: Volunteers tackle trash problem on St. John's highway." *CBC-Radio Canada*, 23 June 2019, cbc.ca/news/canada/newfoundland-labrador/trashy-orr-get-a-clean-up-1.5186892

Editor, Planet. "The 5 Worst Things to Happen to the environment in September 2015." *Planet Experts*, LLC, 30 September 2015, planetexperts.com/the-5-worst-things-to-happen-to-the-environment-in-september-2015/

Editor, Planet. "The 6 Best Things to Happen to the environment in September 2015." *Planet Experts*, LLC, 30 September 2015, planetexperts.com/the-6-best-things-to-happen-to-the-environment-in-september-2015/

Editors, TheFamousPeople.com. "David Suzuki Biography." *TheFamousPeople.com*, thefamouspeople.com/profiles/david-takayoshi-suzuki-1192.php

Gibbens, Sarah. "How the Environment Has Changes Since the First Earth Day. When the first Earth Day was held in 1970, pesticides were killing bald eagles, and soot was darkening the sky. Now, habitat loss and climate change are imperilling the planet." *National Geographic Society*, LLC, 21 April 2018, nationalgeographic.com/news/2018/04/earth-day-then-now-history-science-spd/

Gibbens, Sarah. "15 ways the Trump administration has changed environmental policies. For the past three years, National Geographic has been tracking how this administration's decisions will influence air, water, and wildlife." *National Geographic Society*, LLC, 1 February 2019, nationalgeographic.com/environment/2019/02/15-ways-trump-administration-impacted-environment/

Groom, Nichola. "Special Report: Millions of abandoned oil wells are leaking methane, a climate menace." *Reuters*, 16 June 2020, reuters.com/article/us-usa-drilling-abandoned-specialreport-idUSKBN23N1NL/

Lutkin, Aimee. "A Man Planted A Tree Every Day for 37 Years And Grew A Beautiful Oasis." *Green Matters*, 22 May 2019, greenmatters.com/community/2017/08/21/e7htk/man-plants-tree-every-day-for-37-years

UPI. "U.S. closes last Military base in Canada." *UPI*, Archives, 29 September 1994, upi.com/Archives/1994/09/29/US-closes-last-military-base-in-Canada/7951780811200/

Weidenhammer, Erich. "DEVELOPMENTS IN CANADIAN HYDROMETALLURGY SINCE 1950." *Ingenium*, Canada's Museum of Science and Innovation, March 2021, ingeniumcanada.org/sites/default/files/2021-03/Development_of_Metallurgy_in_Canada_since_1950.pdf

Chapter 3: Conventions

Bradbury, Tara. "UPDATE: Avalon Expo organizer Jeff Power 'is fine,' police say." *Saltwire Network*, 28 August 2017, saltwire.com/newfoundland-labrador/news/update-avalon-expo-organizer-jeff-power-is-fine-police-say-27541/

Harris, Sonia. "Committed Conventions: nearly as much fun as work." *CBR.com,* 24 September 2014, cbr.com/committed-conventions-nearly-as-much-fun-as-work/

Hurley, Cory. "Fat Apollo – Atlanti-Con's adopted superhero." *Saltwire Network,* 30 September 2017, saltwire.com/atlantic-canada/lifestyles/fat-apollo-atlanti-cons-adopted-superhero-141607/

Leigh, Megan. "Why I love conventions: 5 reasons to go to Comin-Con." *PopVerse,* 29 May 2013, pop-verse.com/2013/05/29/why-i-love-conventions/

Loggins, Emma. "Fan Conventions: The Good, the Bad and the Ugly." *FanBolt,* 16 October 2011, fanbolt.com/23679/fan-conventions-the-good-the-bad-and-the-ugly/

Mattu, Ali. "The Good, Bad, and Ugly Psychology of Comic-Con." *brain knows better,* The psychology of science-fiction, 28 May 2014, brainknowsbetter.com/news/2014/5/28/the-good-bad-and-ugly-psychology-of-comic-con

Sweet, Barb. "Fee Fiasco won't stop St. John's sci-fi convention. Troubled Avalon Expo a go this summer in St. John's, Jeff Power says." *Saltwire Network,* 22 February 2018, saltwire.com/newfoundland-labrador/news/local/fee-fiasco-wont-stop-sci-fi-convention-188328/

Chapter 4: Children

Boyle, Louise. "Anxiety over the climate crisis is stopping people having children, study finds." *The Independent UK, Independent Digital News & Media Ltd,* 30 November 2020, independent.co.uk/climate-change/news/climate-crisis-reproduction-children-future-b1763965.html

Gilbert, Sophie. "Why Women Choose Not to Have Children. A detailed in essays by 16 different writers, both male and female: because they don't want to, and because not wanting to is perfectly reasonable." *The Atlantic,* 17 April 2015, theatlantic.com/entertainment/archive/2015/04/why-women-arent-having-children/390765/

Johnson, Matthew. "Want to save your marriage? Don't have kids." *The Guardian, News & Media Limited,* 24 May 2016, theguardian.com/commentisfree/2016/may/24/marriage-kids-children-relationship-suffers-research

Jones, Clare. "Monday Blues – Why do so many people hate their jobs." *ITProPortal, Future Publishing Limited Quay House,* 26 August 2020, itproportal.com/features/monday-blues-why-do-so-many-people-hate-their-jobs

Joshi, Anjali. "100 Reasons Not to Have Kids (That I Discovered After I Had One)." *HuffPost,* 6 December 2017, huffpost.com/entry/100-reasons-not-to-have-kids-that-i-discovered-after-i-had-one_b_5184178

Wikipedia. "Zero population growth." *Wikipedia,* The Free Encyclopedia. 6 May 2021, en.wikipedia.org/wiki/Zero_population_growth

Chapter 5: COVID and the Pandemic

Agency, European Medicines. "COVID-19 Vaccine AstaZeneca: benefits still outweigh the risks despite link to rare blood cloths with low blood platelets." *European Medicines Agency, Sciences Medicines Health,* 18 March 2021, ema.europa.eu/en/news/covid-19-vaccine-astrazeneca-benefits-still-outweigh-risks-despite-possible-link-rare-blood-clots

Alveraz, Lizette. "Opinion: Even by Florida standard, Gov. Ron DeSantis is a covid-19 catastrophe." *The Washington Post,* 21 December 2020, washingtonpost.com/opinions/2020/12/21/ron-desantis-florida-covid-19/

Canada, Health. "Health Canada authorizes use of Pfizer-BioNTech COVID-19 vaccine in children 12 to 15 years of age." *Government of Canada,* 5 May 2021, canada.ca/en/health-canada/news/2021/05/health-canada-authorizes-use-of-the-pfizer-biontech-covid-19-vaccine-in-children-12-to-15-years-of-age.html

Canada, Health. "Approved COVID-19 Vaccines." *Government of Canada,* 2 June 2021, canada.ca/en/health-canada/services/drugs-health-products/covid19-industry/drugs-vaccines-treatments/vaccines.html

Crump, James. "Anti-mask US senator who called virus a hoax tests positive for COVID-19." *Yahoo News, The Independent*, 27 July 2020, ca.news.yahoo.com/anti-mask-us-called-142351086.html

Fears, Darryl. "Amid the pandemic, people are paying more attention to tweets. And not the Twitter kind. A reduction in street noise has created a stage for songbirds." *The Washington Post*, 22 May 202, washingtonpost.com/climate-environment/2020/05/22/amid-pandemic-people-are-paying-more-attention-tweets-not-twitter-kind

Government of Newfoundland and Labrador. "Newfoundland and Labrador Pandemic Update Hub." *Government of Newfoundland and Labrador*, 9 June 2021, covid-19-newfoundland-and-labrador-gnl.hub.arcgis.com

Gross, Samantha. "Is pro wrestling an 'essential business' in Florida? Gov. Ron DeSantis says it is. The statewide stay-at-home order doesn't cover essential businesses. Then the governor layeth down the exception for the WWE." *Tampa Bay Times*, 13 April 2020, tampabay.com/florida-politics/buzz/2020/04/13/is-pro-wrestling-an-essential-business-in-florida-gov-ron-desantis-says-it-is/

IMDb, "Contagion." *Internet Movie Database, An Amazon Company*. 10 April 2020, imdb.com/title/tt1598778/

Li-Men, Yan. Kang, Shu, Guan, Jie, & Hu, Shanchang. (2020, September 14). "Unusual Features of the SARS-CoV-2 Genome Suggesting Sophisticated Laboratory Modification Rather Than Natural Evolution and Delineation of Its Probable Synthetic Route." *Zenodo*, 14 September 2020, doi.org/10.5281/zenodo.4028830

Kaufman, Gil. "Michael Stipe Updates 'It's the End of The World As We Know It' With Coronavirus Survival Tips." *Billboard Music*, 18 March 2020, billboard.com/articles/columns/rock/9337214/michael-stipe-sings-its-the-end-of-the-world-coronavirus-survival-tip

McKenzie, Holly. "Pedestrian-only downtown a hit with residents as St. John's adapts to Pandemic." *CTV News, The Canadian Press*, 11 July 2020, atlantic.ctvnews.ca/pedestrian-only-downtown-a-hit-with-residents-as-st-john-s-adapts-to-pandemic-1.5020270

Peters, Cameron. "A detailed timeline of all the ways Trump failed to respond to the coronavirus." *Vox Media, LLC.* 8 June 2020, vox.com/2020/6/8/21242003/trump-failed-coronavirus-response

Santayana, George. "Those who cannot remember the past are doomed to repeat it." *Dictonary.com,* 27 May 2021, dictionary.com/browse/those-who-cannot-remember-the-past-are-condemned-to-repeat-it

Weiss, Robert. "COVID-19 and the Grief Process. What happens to our differences when our experience is shared?" *Psychology Today*, 30 March 2020, psychologytoday.com/ca/blog/love-and-sex-in-the-digital-age/202003/covid-19-and-the-grief-process

Wikipedia. "Variant of SARS-CoV-2." *Wikipedia*, 10 June 2021, en.wikipedia.org/wiki/Variants_of_SARS-CoV-2

Worldometer, "COVID-19 World Numbers." *Worldometer*, 27 May 2021, worldometers.info/coronavirus/

Chapter 6: Travel

Fears, Darryl. "Amid the pandemic, people are paying more attention to tweets. And not the Twitter kind. A reduction in street noise has created a stage for songbirds." *The Washington Post*, 22 May 2020, washingtonpost.com/climate-environment/2020/05/22/amid-pandemic-people-are-paying-more-attention-tweets-not-twitter-kind

Paudyal, Nabin. "10 Reasons Why Traveling Is The Best Form of Education." *Lifehack*, 24 March 2021, lifehack.org/359773/10-reasons-why-traveling-the-best-form-education

Thompson, Derek. "Should You Give Money to Homeless People?" *The Atlantic*, 22 March 2011, theatlantic.com/business/archive/2011/03/should-you-give-money-to-homeless-people/72820/

Chapter 7: University

Stevenson, Tom. "Going To University Isn't A Waste of Time. A counter-argument to those that say it is, including myself." *Post-Grad Survival*

Guide, Medium. 21 May 2020, medium.com/the-post-grad-survival-guide/going-to-university-isnt-a-waste-of-time-fb8eafba035b

Chapter 8: The Internet

Alexander, John. "The Age of Ignorance." *HuffPost*, 24 August 2017, huffpost.com/entry/the-age-of-ignorance_b_11666646

Barnes, Julian. "Russian Interference in 2020 Included Influencing Trump Associates, Report Says." *The New York Times Company*, 27 May 2021, nytimes.com/2021/03/16/us/politics/election-interference-russia-2020-assessment.html

Culliford, Elizabeth. "TikTok users, K-pop fans say they helped sabotage Trump rally with false registrations." *Reuters*, 21 June 2020, reuters.com/article/us-usa-election-trump-tiktok-idUSKBN23S0L6

Discovery Channel. *CTV, Bell Media*, 27 May 2021, ctv.ca/discovery

Editors, History.com. "Japanese Interment Camps." *A&E Television Networks*, 27 May 2021, history.com/topics/world-war-ii/japanese-american-relocation

ET, "Entertainment Tonight." *CBS Television Studios*, 27 May 2021, etonline.com/

Lee, Bruce. "Trump Once Again Calls Covid-19 Coronavirus the 'Kung Flu'." *Forbes Magazine*, 24 June 2020, forbes.com/sites/brucelee/2020/06/24/trump-once-again-calls-covid-19-coronavirus-the-kung-flu

Li-Men, Yan. Kang, Shu, Guan, Jie, & Hu, Shanchang. "Unusual Features of the SARS-CoV-2 Genome Suggesting Sophisticated Laboratory Modification Rather Than Natural Evolution and Delineation of Its Probable Synthetic Route." *Zenodo*, 14 September 2020, doi.org/10.5281/zenodo.4028830

Mayer, Jane. "How Russia Helped Swing the Election for Trump." The New Yorker, 24 September 2018, newyorker.com/magazine/2018/10/01/how-russia-helped-to-swing-the-election-for-trump

Press, Associated. "Only 23% of Americans have high levels of trust in what Trump is saying about the coronavirus: Poll." *MarketWatch Inc.*, 23 April 2020, marketwatch.com/story/poll-shows-only-23-of-americans-have-high-levels-of-trust-in-what-trump-is-saying-to-the-public-2020-04-23

Riley, Sean. "Net Nanny parental-control app review." *Tom's Guide, Future US Inc.*, 26 August 2020, tomsguide.com/us/zift-app,review-6136.html

Roussletet, M. Duretete, O. Hardouin, M. Grall-Bronnec. "Cult membership: What factors contribute to joining or leaving?" *Psychiatry Research, Elsevier Ireland Ltd.*, 7 November 2017, sciencedirect.com/science/article/pii/S0165178116319941

Spangler, Todd. "Twitter Had Flagged 200 of Trump's Posts as 'Disputed' or Misleading Since Election Day. Does it Make a Difference?" *Variety Media, LLC.*, 27 November 2020, variety.com/2020/digital/news/twitter-trump-200-disputed-misleading-claims-election

Walker, Amanda. "President Trump's use of 'Kung Flu' is embodiment of path he has chosen in divided times. He is president solely for his largely white support base – repeatedly firing with laser focus at their worst instincts." *Sky News UK*, 24 June 2020, news.sky.com/story/president-trumps-use-of-kung-flu-is-embodiment-of-path-he-has-chosen-in-divided-times-12014064

Weekly World News, *Weekly World News*, 26 May 27, 2021, weeklyworldnews.com/

Wikipedia, "Definition of Infotainment." *Wikipedia*, 27 May 2021, en.m.wikipedia.org/wiki/Infotainment

Woodward, Aylin. "A Chinese virologist claimed the coronavirus was 'intentionally' released. Turns out, she works for a group led by Steve Bannon." *Business Insider*, 17 September 2020, businessinsider.com/virologist-who-said-china-released-coronavirus-works-with-steve-bannon-2020-9

Chapter 9: Role-playing Games

Author. "What is D&D? New To The Game." *Wizards of the Coast, Hasbro*, 29 May 2021, dnd.wizards.com/dungeons-and-dragons/what-is-dd

Critical Role. "Crit Role." Critical Role, 18 July 2021, critrole.com/

Miller, Liz. "VIN DIESEL IS A HUGE NERD – AND IT'S MADE HIS MOVIES, FROM FAST & FURIOUS TO BLOODSHOT, SO MUCH BETTER." *SyFy Wire*, 17 March 2020, syfy.com/syfywire/vin-diesel-dungeons-dragons-nerd

Missio, Erik. "How Dungeons And Dragons Can Help With Child Development." *CBC Parents, CBC Radio-Canada*, 15 December 2017, cbc.ca/parents/play/view/how-dungeons-and-dragons-can-help-with-child-development

Novacaska, Melissa. "Geek VS. Verd, WHICH ONE ARE YOU?" *Interrobang, Fanshawe College,* 13 March 2017, theinterrobang.ca/article?aID=13258

Chapter 10: Cycling

BetterHealth. "Cycling – health benefits." *Department of Health, State Government of Victoria, Australia*, 1 January 2020, betterhealth.vic.gov.au/health/healthyliving/cycling-health-benefits

Harvard Health. "The top 5 benefits of Cycling." *Harvard Health Publishing, Harvard Medical School*, 11 August 2016, health.harvard.edu/staying-healthy/the-top-5-benefits-of-cycling

Mazumder, Robin. "Moving Meditation: How Riding A Bike Can Keep You Grounded." *Medium*, 15 January 2019, medium.com/@robinmazumder/movingmeditation-9aa02e52a44c

Chapter 11: Musical Medicine.

Jenkins, Tiffany. "Why does music evoke memories? Songs from the past can stir powerful emotions and transport us back in time." *BBC Culture, BBC,* 21 October 2014, bbc.com/culture/article/20140417-why-does-music-evoke-memories

Naussbaum, Sarah. "Making Music: The tradition of song in the Amish community." *The Daily Record, USA Today Network*, 1 November 2002, the-daily-record.com/article/20021101/NEWS/311019963

Waniata, Ryan. "The Life and Times of the Late, Great CD, Remembering the rise (and final fall) of the late, great Compact Disc." *Digitaltrends, Designtechnica Corporation*, 7 February 2018, digitaltrends.com/features/the-history-of-the-cds-rise-and-fall/

Chapter 12: Relationships

Mejia, Zameena. "Harvard's longest study of adult life reveals how you can be happier and more successful." *CNBC*, 20 March 2018, cnbc.com/2018/03/20/this-harvard-study-reveals-how-you-can-be-happier-and-more-successful.html

Chapter 13: I'm proud to be a Newfoundlander

Bird, Lindsay. "Think N.L. is getting windier? Think again." *CBC Radio-Canada*, 23 January 2019, cbc.ca/news/canada/newfoundland-labrador/newfoundland-labrador-wind-stats-1.4987693

Britannica, Encyclopedia. "Newfoundland and Labrador." *Britannica*, 30 May 2021, britannica.com/place/Newfoundland-and-Labrador/Climate

Buddy Wasisname and the Other Fellers. "Buddy Wassiname and the Other Fellers." *Buddywassisname and the Other Fellers*, 13 January 2018, buddywasisname.com/

Dunn, Stephanie. "12 Fun Facts You Probably Didn't Know About Newfoundland And Labrador." *Narcity, St.Johns*, 22 April 2021, narcity.com/stjohns/12-fun-facts-probably-didnt-know-newfoundland-labrador

Furberg, Anna. "Studded winter tires cost more lives than they save, contribute to global conflict." *Chalmers University of Technology*, 2 October 2018, mdpi.com/1660-4601/15/8/1774/htm

Heritage, Newfoundland and Labrador. "The Provincial Anthem." *Newfoundland and Labrador Heritage, Memorial University of Newfoundland*, 29 May 2021, heritage.nf.ca/articles/society/provincial-anthem.php

Hynes, Ron. "Hynesite." *Hynesite*, 20 December 2015, hynesite.ca

Jansen, Olaf. "The Norse in the North Atlantic." *Newfoundland and Labrador Heritage, Memorial University of Newfoundland*, 1 August 2004, heritage.nf.ca/articles/exploration/norse-north-atlantic.php

Long, Matt. "16 Strange Facts You Should Know About Newfoundland." *Landlopers*, 28 August 2016, landlopers.com/2016/08/28/strange-facts-newfoundland

Moore, Mike. "Remembering Hurricane Igor 10 years later." *CBC Radio-Canada*, 21 September 2020, cbc.ca/news/canada/newfoundland-labrador/hurricane-igor-10-years-later-1.5729975

Oat, Company. "The Oat Company." *Oat Company*, 1 June 2021, oatcompany.com

Roberts, Terry. "Muskrat Falls: A story of unchecked oilmen and their boondoggle hydro project." *CBC Radio-Canada*, 29 April 2019, cbc.ca/news/canada/newfoundland-labrador/muskrat-boondoggle-reasons-1.5088786

Tuck, James. "Beothuk." *The Canadian Encyclopedia, Historica Canada*, 6 February 2006, thecanadianencyclopedia.ca/en/article/beothuk

Yakabuski, Konrad. "Like it or not, natural resources are still the only way forward for Newfoundland." *The Globe and Mail, Phillip Crawley*, 11 May 2021, theglobeandmail.com/business/commentary/article-like-it-or-not-natural-resources-are-still-the-only-way-forward-for/

Chapter 14: The importance of being Vegetarian

Allan, Laura. "17 Times PETA Has Been Criticized For Unethical Behavior." Ranker, *17 August 2020*, ranker.com/list/messed-up-peta-facts/laura-allan

Department of Health. "Vegetarian and vegan eating." *Department of Health, State Government of Victoria, Australia*, 4 June 2021, betterhealth.vic.gov.au/health/healthyliving/vegetarian-and-vegan-eating

Fink, Sheryl. "Could 2020 finally bring an end to the commercial seal hunt in Canada?" *International Fund for Animal Welfare, IFAW*, 8 June 2020, ifaw.org/ca-en/journal/end-commercial-seal-hunt-canada-2020

Hall, Jani. "Demand For Seal Products Has Fallen – So Why Do Canadians Keep Hunting?" *National Geographic, National Geographic Partners, LCC*, 5 April 2017, nationalgeographic.com/animals/article/wildlife-watch-canada-harp-seal-hunt

Harvard Health Publishing. "Becoming a vegetarian." *Harvard Health Publishing, Harvard Medical School*, 15 April 2020, health.harvard.edu/staying-healthy/becoming-a-vegetarian

Harvard Health Publishing. "How to get more probiotics." *Harvard Health Publishing, Harvard Medical School*, 24 August 2020, health.harvard.edu/staying-healthy/how-to-get-more-probiotics

Hoffman, Matthew. "Safer Food For A Healthier You." *WebMD, LLC*, 4 June 2021, webmd.com/diet/features/safer-food-healthier-you#1

Levitt, Tom. "Why Some Farmers Are Ditching Livestock And Growing Plants Instead." *The Huffington Post, HuffPost Impact*, 20 August 2020, huffpost.com/entry/why-farmers-ditching-livestock-growing-plants_n_5e9620b8c5b6a4470cb77646

Meatless Monday. "Go Meatless Monday – It's Good for You, and Good for the Planet." *GRACE Communications Foundation*, 1 June 2021, mondaycampaigns.org/meatless-monday

Roberts, Meg. "Labrador seal hunt largely sidelined as sea ice hits 50-year low." *CBC Radio-Canada*, 12 May 2021, cbc.ca/news/canada/newfoundland-labrador/thin-ice-early-spring-seal-hunt-1.6016897

Sang-Hee, Jeong, Daejin, Kang, Myung-Woon, Lim, Chang Soo, Kang, Ha Jung, Sung. "Risk Assessment of Growth Hormones and Antimicrobial Residues in Meat." *Toxicological Research, The Korean Society of Toxicology*, 1 December 2010, ncbi.nlm.nih.gov/pmc/articles/PMC3834504/

Steber, Carolyn. "11 Surprising Ways Your Body Can Change When You Become A Vegetarian." *Bustle*, 31 January 2018, bustle.com/p/11-surprising-ways-your-body-can-change-when-you-become-a-vegetarian-8058927

Vidal, John. "10 ways vegetarianism can help save the planet." *The Guardian, News & Media Limited*, 18 July 2010, theguardian.com/lifeandstyle/2010/jul/18/vegetarianism-save-planet-environment

Westreich, Sam. "How Does a 1,200 Pound Cow Get Enough Protein?" *Medium*, 27 August 2018, medium.com/a-microbiome-scientist-at-large/how-does-a-1-200-pound-cow-get-enough-protein-506797b53845

Westreich, Sam. "What is a microbiome – a scientist's explanation of how our newest organ affects us." *Medium*, 31 July 2018, medium.com/@westwise/what-is-a-microbiome-a-scientists-explanation-of-how-our-newest-organ-affects-us-ac04c22d4b49

Chapter 15: Losing a Parent

Jones, Clare. "Monday Blues – Why do so many people hate their jobs." *ITProPortal, Future Publishing Limited Quay House*, 26 August 2020, itproportal.com/features/monday-blues-why-do-so-many-people-hate-their-jobs

Krisch, Joshua. "The Death of a Parent Affects Even Grown Children Psychologically and Physically." *Health and Science, Fatherly*, 2 May 2021, fatherly.com/health-science/parent-death-psychological-physical-effects/

Dawson, Alene. "What the death of a parent can teach us, if we're willing to learn." *Los Angeles Times*, 19 January 2018, latimes.com/health/la-he-death-of-a-parent-20180120-story.html

Chapter 16: The Geeks Will Inherit the Earth

Harrison, Andrew. "Rise of the new geeks: how the outsiders won." *The Guardian, News & Media Limited*, 2 September 2013, theguardian.com/fashion/2013/sep/02/rise-geeks-outsiders-superhero-movies-dork

Jones, Clare. "Monday Blues – Why do so many people hate their jobs." *ITProPortal, Future Publishing Limited Quay House*, 26 August 2020, itproportal.com/features/monday-blues-why-do-so-many-people-hate-their-jobs

Vary, Adam. "Emmys: 'WandaVision,' 'The Boys' Lead Historic Year for Comic Book Adapations." *Variety*, Media, LLC, 13 July 2021, variety.com/2021/tv/news/emmys-wandavision-the-boys-falcon-winter-soldier-marvel-studios

Wikipedia. "The Lord of the Rings." *Wikipedia, The Free Encyclopedia.* 23 June 2021, en.wikipedia.org/wiki/The_Lord_of_the_Rings

Acknowledgements

I want to say thank you my wife, Joanne, quite literally I would not have been able to write this book without her as she is the most important addition to my life these past 21 years. She is my best friend, my greatest love and the most special person I know, I love her more every day and will continue to do so for the rest of my life. I can be a handful and I continue to feel lucky every day to be loved by you.

Thanks to all my family for everything you have done for me and continue to help me out when I need it. Thank you to the reader of this book, while it is an untraditional one, I suppose writer and reader do have a relationship. I am lucky to have one reader, Andrew who lives in Florida, that has read most of my books and even came here to visit me (and to see Newfoundland of course), that was a great experience that I look back fondly on.

Thank you to my mom for always being there for me. She is a wonderful Mom, grandmother and continues to surprise me as she changes and grows in her senior years.

Thank you to all the fans of my writing, I hope you enjoy my first attempt at non-fiction and continue to follow me on my writing journey.

Next, I'd like to promote my publishing group, Four Phoenixes Publishing, and I hope that when you're done with this book, you'll consider reading other great novels by Jennifer L. Gadd, Joe Chianakas, and Kevin Wright.

I want to thank my editor, Heather Reilly. Heather continues to be an absolute professional and is a joy to work with. This book she went above and beyond discussing each chapter with me in detail and showing me what worked and what did not. I find it is always extremely important to get the perspective of another writer, a woman and a reasonable person (which I don't always claim to be). She has complimented and encouraged me to keep writing and I look forward to working with her again in the future.

My friend John was a huge help with some final editing and formatting, he has also always been a great sounding board, both of which are greatly appreciated.

I love to hear from my fans so please feel free to contact me through my website.

Until next time, remember that things are never as bad as they seem, and every dark cloud really does have a silver lining. The world isn't coming to an end, it's just time for a (well-needed) shakeup, what's comes next will be better, I just know it.

Charles O'Keefe,
June 2021.

About the Author: Charles O'Keefe

Charles O'Keefe lives in the beautiful province of Newfoundland, Canada, with his wife and two feline 'children,' Lucy and Eleanor. He is a part-owner of a beauty wholesale business. He enjoys many hobbies and activities that include reading, gaming, poker, Pilates, bike riding, Dungeons and Dragons, going to conventions and updating his blog. Charles is the author of four books in the *Newfoundland Vampire* series and a collection of short stories. Along with this non-fiction book currently in your hands/onscreen.

To find out more about Charles or his other books, go to Twitter and Facebook or visit his web site at:

CharlesOkeefe.com

Other books by Charles O'Keefe:

The Newfoundland Vampire Book I
The Newfoundland Vampire Book II: Killer on the Road
The Newfoundland Vampire Book III: The Gathering Dark
The Newfoundland Vampire Book IV: War of the Fangs
The Chaos Stories: Tales of Magic, Terror, Passion and Blood.

Find out more about the author and his books on:

Twitter
Facebook
Goodreads

And on his website at:

CharlesOkeefe.com

www.ingramcontent.com/pod-product-compliance
Lightning Source LLC
Chambersburg PA
CBHW060506030426
42337CB00015B/1768